Problem–Based Learning Innovation

Using Problems to Power Learning in the 21st Century

OON-SENG TAN

D0161001

CENGAGE
Learning™

Australia • Brazil • Japan • Korea • Mexico • Singapore • Spain • United Kingdom • United States

CENGAGE
Learning™

Problem-Based Learning Innovation: Using Problems to Power Learning in the 21st Century

Oon-Seng Tan

Publishing Director:
Paul Tan

Assistant Publishing Manager:
Pauline Lim

Senior Product Director:
Janet Lim

Senior Product Manager:
Charles Ho

© 2003 Cengage Learning Asia Pte Ltd

ALL RIGHTS RESERVED. No part of this work covered by the copyright herein may be reproduced, transmitted, stored or used in any form or by any means graphic, electronic, or mechanical, including but not limited to photocopying, recording, scanning, digitalizing, taping, Web distribution, information networks, or information storage and retrieval systems, without the prior written permission of the publisher.

For permission to use material from this text or product, email to
asia.publishing@cengage.com

ISBN-13: 978-981-243-717-4
ISBN-10: 981-243-717-7

Cengage Learning Asia Pte Ltd
5 Shenton Way #01-01
UIC Building
Singapore 068808

Cengage Learning is a leading provider of customized learning solutions with office locations around the globe, including Singapore, the United Kingdom, Australia, Mexico, Brazil and Japan.

Locate your local office at: **international.cengage.com/region**

Cengage Learning products are represented in Canada by Nelson Education, Ltd.

For product information, visit **cengageasia.com**

Printed in Singapore
5 6 7 8   11 10 09 08

CONTENTS

FOREWORD

I first met Oon-Seng Tan when he visited my centre at Stanford University in 1997. He was then working as a staff developer and his passion for improving teaching and learning in higher education impressed me deeply.

In 2000 I was invited by Oon-Seng, in his capacity as chairman of the International Advisory Committee for the Second Asia-Pacific Conference on Problem-based Learning (APCPBL), to be the conference keynote speaker. That year he was Director of the Temasek Centre for Problem-based Learning and received an Innovator Award from the Enterprise Challenge Unit (Prime Minister's Office, Singapore) for co-pioneering a project on problem-based learning (PBL). His receipt of this award was not surprising as I had seen the dedication and the creative energy of Oon-Seng and his colleagues at Temasek when I was an International Advisor there in 1998.

Amazingly and encouragingly, the modest yet powerful idea of PBL continues to bring educators together from across the globe each year. I understand that the Third APCPBL was held in Australia in 2001, the fourth in Thailand in 2002 and the fifth will be held in Malaysia. In the United States, PBL has also gained additional momentum and has increasingly been recognized as an important innovation in primary, secondary and post-secondary curricula.

As someone who has worked extensively with PBL projects at various levels of education, Oon-Seng is especially well positioned to understand the needs of educators in attempting to use PBL approaches. His expertise in staff development, teacher education and psychology enables him to provide a fresh perspective on how problems can be used as starting points to power student learning in new ways. This book illustrates how PBL can be used holistically to cater to curiosity, inquiry, self-directed learning and collaborative learning. Such key ideas as design of problems, design of learning environments, coaching and facilitation techniques, implementation models and assessment in PBL are addressed.

I congratulate Associate Professor Oon-Seng Tan on the insights in this book and highly recommend it to educators worldwide who are interested in innovating their curricula.

Michele Marincovich PhD
Associate Vice Provost for Undergraduate Education
Director, Center for Teaching and Learning
Stanford University

PREFACE

The new millennium is characterized by unprecedented breakthroughs in knowledge and technology. To meet 21st century challenges, in what ways can educators incorporate real-world problems, higher-order thinking skills, multidisciplinary learning, independent learning, information mining, teamwork and communication skills into their curricula? In their attempts to innovate learning, many educators have discovered the value of problem-based learning (PBL) approaches.

When I chaired the International Advisory Committee of the Second Asia-Pacific Conference on Problem-based Learning (APCPBL) in 2000, I did not expect the momentum of the use of PBL to pick up and extend so rapidly within such a short time to so many countries. It has been encouraging to see the interest in PBL at the Third APCPBL in Australia, the International Conference on University Learning and Teaching in Malaysia, and the International Conference on Problem-based Learning in Higher Education in Baltimore, USA, where I was privileged to be invited to deliver keynote addresses.

Interest in using PBL has surged in numerous training institutions and secondary schools in Singapore and the region. The implementation of PBL approaches is a challenging task and we need to have a better understanding of PBL in the light of pedagogical and psychological developments.

This book explains why PBL has become an innovation in education. More importantly, it aims to provide educators and practitioners with an updated and holistic perspective of how we may practically infuse PBL into curricula. The ideas are gleaned from the many PBL trials and implementations and are a result of learning from many PBL projects across disciplines and educational levels.

The chapters focus on the following areas:

- Chapter 1: the big picture of educational challenges and the relevance of PBL
- Chapter 2: the "whys" of PBL from developments in pedagogy and insights drawn from psychology
- Chapter 3: characteristics of PBL and illustrations of the PBL cycle
- Chapter 4: PBL processes and examples of how to facilitate the various key stages

- Chapter 5: infusion of higher-order thinking and cognitive coaching
- Chapter 6: design of PBL problems
- Chapter 7: curriculum goals, structure and assessment of PBL
- Chapter 8: using Internet communication technologies in PBL and e-learning
- Chapter 9: understanding the needs of students and their experiences in PBL
- Chapter 10: pointers for implementing PBL projects

I hope this book will contribute to the advancement of the knowledge and practice in the use of PBL approaches as well as stir up interest and new attempts to innovate classroom practices and curricula.

Oon-Seng Tan PhD
Associate Professor and Head of Psychological Studies
National Institute of Education
Nanyang Technological University
Singapore

ACKNOWLEDGEMENTS

I was privileged to explore, investigate and pilot a variety of problem-based learning (PBL) approaches with enthusiastic academic staff from different disciplines when I was Director of the Temasek Centre for Problem-based Learning. When I took up a professorial post at Nanyang Technological University, one of the first things I was requested to do was to give a talk on PBL and collaborative learning on the Teaching Excellence Award Day for Nanyang staff. I was heartened by the support from Professor S. Gopinathan, Associate Professor Esther Tan, Associate Professor Agnes Chang, Dr Ang Wai Hoong and the academic staff of Psychological Studies, National Institute of Education, when I introduced PBL into one of the core modules pertaining to educational psychology. I would like to thank the many staff members, colleagues and students involved in the various PBL programmes.

My thanks go to Dr N. Varaprasad, then Chief Executive Officer of Temasek Polytechnic and now Deputy President of the National University of Singapore, who has been most visionary in educational innovation – from him, I actually learnt how to use PBL in management. Many thanks to numerous friends who taught me PBL, kept me in the international loop of PBL and got me involved in conferences, research and publications on PBL. Michele Micetich, Director of the Center for Problem-based Learning at the Illinois Mathematics and Science Academy, gave me my first personal tutoring on PBL. Dr Martin Ramirez, Chief Learning Officer of IDEAS at Naperville, shared with me his insights into what can be done with PBL. Penny Little and Jane Conway, who initiated PROBLARC in Australia, taught me how to do staff development in PBL. Professor Anthony Dixon (University of Hong Kong), Professor Tadahiko Kozu (Tokyo Women Medical University), Professor Donald Woods (McMaster University), Dr De Gallow (University of California, Irvine), Professor S.D. Patki (Colombo Plan Staff College), Ranald Macdonald (Sheffield Hallam University) and Professor S.U.K. Ekaratne (University of Colombo) supported my APCPBL initiatives. Professor George Watson (University of Delaware), Mary Sue Baldwin (Director, Center for Problem-based Learning at Samford), Professor Hazadiah Mohd Dahan (Universiti Teknologi MARA), Dr William Wu (Hong Kong Baptist University), Professor Colin Power (UNESCO),

Associate Professor Esther Daniel (University of Malaya), Dr Peter Mack (Chairman, Medical Pedagogy Committee, Postgraduate Medical Institute, Singapore General Hospital) and many others keep me learning by involving me in their PBL initiatives, conferences and in their work to improve learning worldwide.

My thanks to Temasek Polytechnic and members of the Law team, comprising Cynthia Lim Ai Ming, Linda Tan, Eileen Ng and Lim Ting Yin, for generously allowing me to cite a PBL example from their highly innovative course. Thanks to my Postgraduate Diploma in Higher Education group, in particular June Khor of Nanyang Polytechnic and Jerry Soo of Nanyang Academy of Fine Arts, for their PBL cases. Special thanks to the many involved in my PBL workshops for schools. I have learnt so much from them. My thanks to Hee Piang Chin, Assistant Director at the Ministry of Education, for her continued support of training programmes in PBL for teachers. Thanks to Kon Mei Leen, Principal of Methodist Girls' School, and her enthusiastic teachers Clarissa Tan, Wendy Ng and Celine Teo, who enabled me to see in-depth how PBL can be developed and infused into secondary school curricula. Thanks to Jennifer Choy, Principal of St Anthony's Canossian Secondary School, Vice-Principal Chua Bee Leng and their staff for giving me the opportunity to see their PBL innovations.

This publication would not be possible without the enthusiastic support of Paul Tan (Director of Publishing), Jessica Chan, Ivy Yeo and the many capable staff at Thomson Learning. My special thanks to Ang Lee Ming for her excellent editing.

My heartfelt thanks to Dr Michele Marincovich, Associate Vice Provost of Stanford University, who willingly took time from her busy and tight schedule to write the Foreword.

Last but not least, my dear wife, Kek Joo, and our sons, Zhong Xing and Chen Xing, gave me much joy and support with their humour, encouragement and cheer for me to go on punching the keys to bring my thoughts to fruition.

1

MEETING 21ST CENTURY NEEDS IN EDUCATION

Problems and Intelligences

Education in this 21st century is about developing intelligences.

A story was told about a prospective university student deciding which course to take. The student asked a college student adviser to recommend a course of study that would ensure "a job with a future". The adviser told the student: "All jobs have no future; just study what you think you will enjoy." Indeed, jobs have no future; only people have future – people with the intelligences to craft their careers and future by relentless pursuit and creative learning.

Professor Howard Gardner of Harvard University, one of the foremost psychologists of our times, described intelligence as the ability to solve problems in one's particular context and culture. Noted for his theory of multiple intelligences, Gardner (1983) argued for the notion of intelligence as a multiple reality and identified several distinct ways of learning and knowing reality that he described as intelligences. The seven commonly cited intelligences are verbal, logical–mathematical, visual–spatial, bodily–kinesthetic, musical, interpersonal, and intrapersonal intelligences. Nothing manifests the need for these multiple intelligences more than the challenge of dealing with real-world problems.

Many educators support the need to develop multiple intelligences, but few realize that one of the best ways to draw forth these intelligences is to make use of problem scenarios.

> Developing intelligence is about learning to solve problems. Problem solving in real-world contexts involves multiple ways of knowing and learning.

Intelligence in the real world involves not only learning how to do things and actually doing them, but also the ability to deal with novelty as well as the capacity to adapt, select and shape our interactions with the environment (Sternberg, 1985, 1986, 1990). The importance of understanding the many components and dimensions of intelligence and developing intelligence has been repeatedly emphasized by Robert Sternberg, IBM Professor at Yale University. It is therefore not surprising that Sternberg is also one of the strongest proponents for changes in the current educational practices.

In Singapore, a S$10 million fund was established in 1999 under the auspices of the Prime Minister's Office to provide "venture capital" for innovative and enterprising projects (the funding has since expanded). Known as the Enterprise Challenge, the goal then was to fund innovations that would create new value or significant improvement in public services in Singapore. It was a modest initiative to highlight new mindsets needed to meet the challenges of the knowledge economy. One of the first to win the award, in 2000, was an educational development project on problem-based learning, of which I was a co-pioneer (Tan, 2002d). When making our case for the award before the panel, I was quizzed on why such an educational innovation was important. One of my arguments was that it was not just about extending the spectrum of educational methodologies, but our innovation was addressing a change in paradigm – the way we look at knowledge and the way people should relook at learning given the accessibility of knowledge and the information explosion. Singapore had already invested heavily in creating one of the best information technology (IT) hubs and becoming one of the most wired cities in the world. Optimizing the use of the IT infrastructure, however, involves more than using e-mail and retrieving information.

Problem-based learning (PBL) is about harnessing the kinds of intelligences needed in confronting real-world challenges: the ability to deal with novelty and complexity (Tan, 2000c). This book is about the why, what and how of PBL.

> **Education in the 21st century is about dealing with new real-world problems. PBL approaches involve harnessing intelligences from within individuals, from groups of people and from the environment to solve problems that are meaningful, relevant and contextualized.**

Reflecting on Our Educational Practices

Since PBL always begins with a problem, we should perhaps begin likewise. Consider the following problem:

In our current educational practices, are we developing students with the necessary intelligences and capabilities for the 21st century? What are the challenges facing your current education system?

You may like to jot down some of your reflections before you continue reading.

In many of my presentations, lectures and workshops, I often highlight that educators today need to ask not only the "how" questions but also the "why". I would like to suggest that educators increasingly think in terms of the 3Ps:

- Paradigms (What are our worldviews?)
- Philosophy (What are our beliefs?)
- Practicality (What do we do?)

Our worldview must be both telescopic and helicopter in nature. By telescopic I mean understanding the past (where we came from and how we arrived at the present) and seeing into the future (intelligent extrapolation). We also need a helicopter view of things: rising above micro and fragmentary issues and having a big picture of things. We need the appropriate paradigms with the right worldviews and the right assumptions. Kuhn (1962) was probably the first to use the term *paradigm* through his work *The Structure of Scientific Revolutions*. He was alluding to the existence of a conflict of worldviews where there was a need to shift our underlying assumptions about things.

As educators, we operate with many assumptions. For example:

- What are our assumptions about knowledge and how it should be best transmitted?
- How do we look at knowledge and information today?
- We have many assumptions about our role as teachers. Do teachers see themselves primarily as subject teachers (content disseminators) or more?
- How do teachers view their interaction with the knowledge milieu?
- We have our assumptions about how students learn. What are our assumptions about student participation?
- Do we see students as merely knowledge recipients?

- What are our assumptions about empowering others to acquire knowledge?
- What are our assumptions about how we should prepare our students for the future?

Both the end in mind (the desired outcomes) and the journey are important. We need to know the kinds of outcomes that we want in terms of competencies and intelligences needed to function in the 21st century.

Reflecting on Changes around Us

On a trip to Silicon Valley in California with a team of educators, we visited the headquarters of Oracle Corporation at Redwood Shores. An Oracle executive remarked confidently: "The Internet is great – but we create the software that powers the Internet." Oracle is of course well known worldwide for its Web-based databases, tools and applications. In Singapore, we are often proud of the fact that we have invested much time and effort in planning for many aspects of life, including education. It dawned on me, however, that education is not just about preparing students for the future. An aphorism in Silicon Valley is that "we don't predict the future; we invent it".

What kind of educational paradigm do we need so that our students will be equipped not just to cope with the future but also to power or even invent it?

Consider the following world trends and think in terms of how they might impact on our preparation of students for the future?

- Worldwide economic competitiveness
- Changes in the economic and financial scenes
- New political landscapes
- Changes in the social scene
- Changes in industrial demands
- Changes in business and services
- New patterns of consumer behaviour
- Globalization
- IT trends
- Proliferation of innovations
- Changes in workplace demands
- Changing expectations of employers

We live in a new millennium characterized by unprecedented breakthroughs in knowledge and technology. To cope with the changes in many aspects of life, we need to prepare students with a different set of intelligences to function effectively in a new world. Traditional notions of the

Education is not just about preparing people for the future; it is also about inventing our future.

transmission of knowledge, skills and attitudes seem inadequate to address this need. There is an urgent need for educators to recognize the implications of these dynamic changes.

Global and National Agendas for Educational Reform

Most leaders and policy makers know that for a nation to succeed we need to encourage members of the society to achieve their educational potentials. The nature of education and its curricula has implications not only for the quality of life but also for the creation of national wealth (Tan, 1996, 1999). Many nations grapple with their national educational agendas to align curriculum practices with the need for national and global survival from social, economic and political perspectives.

In Asia, the need to refine education systems to foster creative thinking, entrepreneurial spirit and lifelong learning has been repeatedly articulated. The daily news is flooded with talk about the knowledge-based economy (KBE), the rapid proliferation of IT, information accessibility, new industrial and business challenges, and changing political and social landscapes. For example, the *Straits Times* on 12 November 2002 carried the headline: "Panel on workers wants school reforms". The article noted a high-level panel advocating reforming the education system, starting at the secondary school level, in order to propel the Singapore economy in the future.

Faced with the choice of old and new, educators have a tendency to cling to the old. Some of us would often try to prove at the end of the day that we were right not to jump onto the bandwagon of unproven methods and paradigms. For some educators, change merely implies adding more new things without discarding the old.

Perhaps some of these behaviours are reinforced by previous experiences. The initial advent of computers, for example, led to the introduction of computer-aided instruction and computer-based learning, but these had little impact on the overall educational systems and processes. They were just advancement of educational technologies and, like educational television and video, merely broadened the repertoire of delivery modes and the range of instructional technologies. Their adoption was not a serious concern as their impact, when compared with traditional methods of classroom teaching, was not significant. These earlier waves did not have quantum-leap implications and did not call for drastic revamp of education.

Changes today are, however, of a different nature altogether. The Internet era has implications far beyond the realm of instructional technology. Information access and retrieval is at the click of a mouse. There is a serious need to relook at our assumptions of knowledge acquisition and participation in learning. The role of teachers as authority in specific fields of knowledge has been eroded. The dissemination of knowledge may no longer be of primary importance at some stages of education as the World Wide Web provides ready information anytime anywhere. The role of teachers will have to change dramatically if it is to remain relevant to a new generation of students. In fact, the Internet revolution calls for a revamp in curriculum content, delivery and assessment.

How should education address the issues of knowledge management and prepare our students for this knowledge era?

There are of course many things that educators are doing right, and we do not want to throw out the baby with the bath water. In Asia, schools are quite good at getting students to learn a mammoth amount of information and problem-solving routines through memorization and imitation. Education, however, needs to address issues not only of doing things right but of doing the right things right.

Figure 1.1 illustrates the shift needed to address change today. From "doing things right", one needs to move on to learning to do the "right things right". There is a need for creative destruction and innovation – discarding things that are efficient but are no longer effective in a new environment. In the 1970s when working as a military reporter, I was greatly impressed with the press typists. These ladies had great mastery and dexterity with their typewriters and their work was almost always flawless. They had to type on three sheets of a typing paper with carbon copies. They were so superb both in speed and accuracy that they hardly had to make corrections, unless my written draft was wrong or illegible. They were people who did things right. But what has happened to their highly efficient work? They may have had done everything right, but what they did then is now an obsolete process. The right thing for them to do now is of course to use the computer. The advent of the computer enhances productivity in writing and publishing immensely. Possessing word processing skills

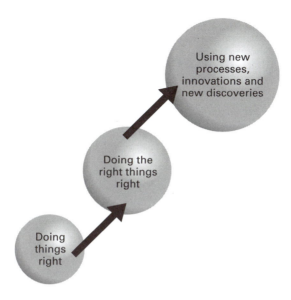

Figure 1.1 Paradigm shift towards change

is, however, still not good enough. The typist's role is obsolete and typists need to continually learn new software and creatively use these new capabilities to do multiple functions as administrative support if they want to be employable. Similarly, educators today need to assume new roles, such as being designers of the learning environment.

The Committee on Singapore Competitiveness observed that over the last three decades Singapore has had a successful education system that supported a production-based economy (Ministry of Trade and Industry, 1998). However, to "improve the longer-term competitiveness of Singapore, we should refine our education system to help

> **Educators today are not just disseminators of information or even facilitators. Learning has to extend beyond the physical boundary of the classroom and educators need to become designers of the learning environment.**

foster creative thinking and entrepreneurial spirit among the young" (p. 86). It recommended that three major components of the education system should be addressed:

- the content of the curriculum
- the mode of delivering this curriculum to students
- the assessment of performance

The Economic Development Board similarly emphasized that for "our knowledge-based economy to flourish, we will need a culture which encourages creativity and entrepreneurship, as well as an appetite for change and risk-taking" (1999, 3).

Figures 1.2 and 1.3 depict the shift in preoccupation as we move towards a KBE. To cope with the shift, it is not good enough to have an education system that prides on developing people with strong competencies in analytical, systematic and systems thinking. The KBE calls for new competencies. In Singapore, for example, the concern

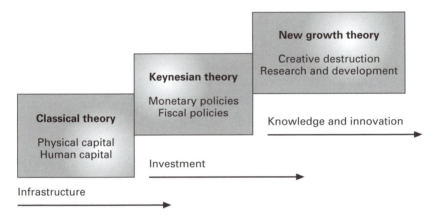

Figure 1.2 The knowledge-based economy

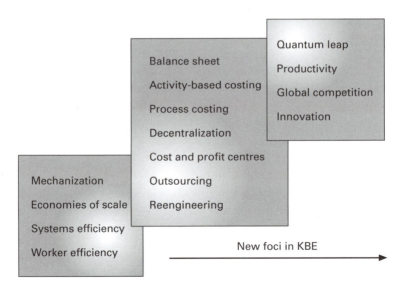

Figure 1.3 New foci of preoccupation in the knowledge-based economy (KBE)

with "keeping pace with changes in the world" was repeatedly emphasized by the Ministry of Education (*Straits Times*, 31 July 1997, p. 1). The desired outcomes of education for post-secondary students were redefined to include characteristics such as the ability to think, reason and deal confidently with the future; to seek, process and apply knowledge; innovativeness; a spirit of continual improvement; a lifelong habit of learning; and an enterprising spirit in undertakings (Ministry of Education, 1998, 4).

The aim of *Manpower 21: Vision of a Talent Capital*, the strategic blueprint for developing Singapore's manpower, is to turn Singapore into a place "where people use their talents to create value; where entrepreneurs abound and thrive; and in which people can develop and multiply their potential through continuous learning and participation in meaningful jobs. It is a centre of ideas, innovation, knowledge and exchange; a place with a strong culture of continuous learning for lifelong employability" (Ministry of Manpower, 1999, 18). The report noted that the reasons for lifelong learning are strong, but it observed that "the majority of our working population do not pursue any form of training" (p. 24).

More revolutionary changes are thus needed in curricula and in education (Tan, 2000c). My observations concur with those of Dr Tony Tan, Deputy Prime Minister of Singapore, that education is in need of a major overhaul; in fact, he noted that incremental change is not favoured as it would just "aggravate the problem of perpetuating practices that should be jettisoned if a country is to move ahead" (*Straits Times*, 2002, p. H2).

Corollaries of the above concerns include changing the mindsets of both the present and the future generations in learning to learn, the need for continuous learning, assuming personal responsibility for one's own learning, and embracing new approaches of learning that prepare individuals with relevant competencies.

In a university survey, employers ranked as most important the following eight competencies: teamwork, problem solving, ability to take initiative, desire to learn, interpersonal skills, ability to work independently, oral communication, and flexibility in applying knowledge (National University of Singapore, 2000). To what extent do current modes of training, teaching and learning equip people with the necessary competencies and skills?

Learning in the Knowledge-based Economy

Education must foster the creation of a critical mass of individuals with greater creativity and higher levels of thinking skills. Education would fail if institutions continue to teach content to students without paying attention to how quickly such content knowledge becomes obsolete or irrelevant (Brennan et al., 1999). Educators need to ask if the skills imparted are really transferable to the workplace. Teachers would have failed if they use learning processes that do not impact on lifelong learning.

Figure 1.4 shows how changes through quantum-leap innovation differ from incremental changes produced using an existing process. The idea of innovation in the KBE is to discard something not because it is not producing results but because, though it may be efficient, it is not necessarily effective today (like typists and their typewriters). We are often caught in the paradigm of producing more of the same. Do we really need to reinvent our educational practices to meet the challenges of the KBE?

Earlier you were asked to reflect on our current educational practices. Look at the following practices and indicate the extent to which each of these practices is prevalent in your curriculum:

- Student-independent learning
- Information mining

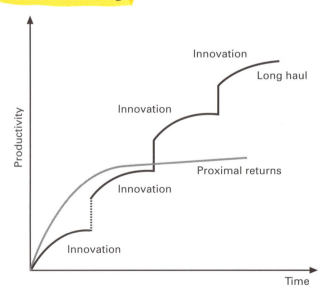

Figure 1.4 Quantum-leap changes through innovation

- Use of real-world challenges
- Use of unstructured problems
- Contextualization of content knowledge
- Use of higher-order thinking skills
- Students defining scope and issues of learning
- Peer teaching
- Peer evaluation
- Teamwork
- Multidisciplinary learning
- Assessment of process skills

The challenge is indeed for educators to design new learning milieus and curricula that really encourage motivation and independence so as to equip students with learning, thinking and problem-solving skills. Knapper and Cropley (1991) observed that "to cope with the demands of a rapidly changing world we need an educated population, capable of taking the initiative for their own education, and motivated to continue learning throughout their lives and in many different situations" (p. 7). Schlechty (1990) observed that existing secondary school structures with single-subject, single-classroom, single-teacher formats lack generative and meaningful collaborative learning. Hargreaves (1994) noted the need for teachers and schools to educate young people in skills and qualities like adaptability, responsibility, flexibility and capacity to work with others.

Our paradigms may be correct, but if we do not believe that we can move on and succeed in that paradigm then we would again be stuck. Teachers need to believe that innovation in education is necessary and can work. Educators themselves – principals and teachers – must be more entrepreneurial in trying new approaches to learning.

Education in the KBE should involve:

- encouraging lifelong learning (learning throughout life)
- fostering lifewide learning (transfer of learning across contexts and disciplines)
- assuming greater personal responsibility for one's learning
- learning how to learn from multiple sources and resources
- learning collaboratively
- learning to adapt and to solve problems (i.e. to cope with change)

A Model for Curriculum Shift

The term *curriculum* refers not only to the intended learning outcomes but also to the environment for bringing about these outcomes. Looking at a curriculum thus involves consideration of all the experiences that individual learners have in a programme of education (Parkay & Hass, 2000) as well as the design of the learning environment (Tan, 1994).

Tan (2000c) argued for a curriculum shift of three foci of preoccupation as illustrated in Figure 1.5. Traditional programmes of education and training have an over-preoccupation with content. What is important is a shift towards designing more real-world problems as anchors around which learners achieve the learning outcomes through the process of actively working on unstructured problems. In many ways, this calls for a problem-based approach to the curriculum. It has been argued that by using "real-life" problems as a focus learners would really learn how to learn. Boud and Feletti (1997) noted that PBL is the most significant innovation in education. It suffices at this stage to say that by having real-life problems (rather than content) as focal points, learners as active problem solvers and teachers as mediating coaches, the learning paradigm would shift towards attainment of outcomes desired in a knowledge-based era. Margetson (1994) noted that a PBL curriculum helps promote the development of lifelong learning skills in the form of open-minded, reflective, critical and active learning. Furthermore, it has been observed that PBL curricula can better facilitate the acquisition of problem-solving, communication, teamwork and interpersonal skills – attributes that are sought after by industry.

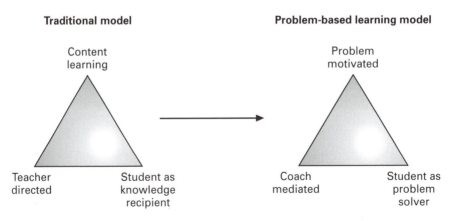

Figure 1.5 A model of curriculum shift

Arguments dealing with what counts as knowledge are not new (Brennan et al., 1999; Tan, 2002e). Taking an overly simplistic approach, I shall define the need for content knowledge as "knowing what" and for process knowledge as "knowing why and how", borrowing Schon's ideas in *The Reflective Practitioner*. The argument is for the teaching of processes and the use of real-world scenarios in learning. The implications for teaching and learning are that teachers should be:

- designers of learning
- facilitators and mediators of learning

It is not how much content we disseminate in our classrooms but how we engage students' motivation and independent learning that is important. In PBL, the design of real-world problem scenarios is crucial and the problems act as triggers for self-directed and collaborative learning. If we want to develop more entrepreneurship, students need to learn to take greater ownership of their learning – particularly the acquisition of facts. There are difficult challenges in such educational approaches: handling large numbers of students, students schooled with the mindset of dependence on digested information and didactics, and inadequacies of reading skills. Learning to learn and lifelong learning are important goals. There will be increasing demands in the future for workers to be able to read more prolifically and to write and communicate confidently.

As facilitators and mediators of learning, our role is to teach heuristics, provide scaffolding and connect students to the milieu of knowledge available in texts, various other sources and the World Wide Web. The design of the learning environment would need to include opportunities for the development of collaborative learning.

Methods of assessment will also have to change. Teachers and students are heavily engaged with examinations. Charles Handy (1994) described what he called the Macnamara Fallacy as something like this: We measure what is easily measured and disregard what we cannot easily measure. Then we presume what can't be measured as unimportant, and we assume what can't be measured as non-existent. He described this as suicidal. Many of the competencies and process skills cannot be easily measured. Examinations that primarily test content knowledge are deemed as most reliable and objective, but the assessment of content knowledge alone may lack validity in today's world. Eraut (1994), for example, highlighted that, whilst a written syllabus may acknowledge skills such as "communication" and "learning to work in teams" as basic and important, in reality the learning processes used do not cater to these developments. Writing a good essay on "interpersonal skills" does not necessarily reflect knowledge about people, working with people and real situations.

> **In the KBE, we need to learn to solve novel problems, to assume personal responsibility for learning, to learn collaboratively and from multiple resources, and to be able to transfer learning across disciplines and contexts.**

In today's world of knowledge and participation, assessment should be more about learning rather than selection. Diversification of assessment appears to be essential to broadening learning, and implementation of more innovative learning methods such as PBL and project work must be complemented by more holistic reviews of the curriculum and evaluation.

We also need the practicality and the know-how – otherwise we will be caught up in plenty of discussions, seminars and workshops without translating things into action and without really bringing about change.

In this Internet era, how we learn is what we learn. Are we designing the learning environment and facilitating learning that motivate students to learn in ways that empower them for tomorrow? Or are we escaping the responsibility of tomorrow by evading changes in our practices?

In the chapters that follow, we will reveal how the infusion of PBL approaches into the curriculum, as well as its associated innovations pertaining to areas such as collaborative learning, cross-disciplinary learning and the use of e-resources, provides possibilities in the quest for educational reform.

2

PROBLEMS, PEDAGOGY AND PROBLEM-BASED LEARNING

The Power of Problems

In a life science class, a teacher begins a lesson by posing a problem scenario:

How is it that when an apple drops on the floor some parts of it get damaged and turn brown? Why is that an orange does not turn brown when it is similarly hit?

The students' curiosity is further aroused when told that some 80 years ago a scientist asked a similar question: Why does a banana turn brown when it is hit? They are told that the scientist became so fascinated with and so immersed in the "banana problem" that he eventually won a Nobel Prize!

The teacher proceeds to give hints and questions for discussion that lead to the content to be learnt. The students eventually obtain several sources of references and find the information and solution to the problem.

The scientist was a Hungarian named Albert Szent-Gyorgyi. To solve the problem, Szent-Gyorgyi reasoned by comparing, classifying, observing and connecting key information in biology and chemistry. He came up with the idea that there are two categories of plants: those that turn brown on being damaged and those that do not. The fact is that plants have compounds called polyphenols. When plant or fruit tissues are damaged, the polyphenols react with oxygen to form the brown or black colour. Szent-Gyorgyi discovered that fruits like oranges contain rather large amounts of a certain sugar-like compound. He succeeded in isolating this compound, which he named ascorbic acid (vitamin C). The presence of vitamin C prevents oxygen from oxidizing the polyphenols into brown compounds. Dr Szent-Gyorgyi's work on the biological combustion processes pertaining to vitamin C won him the Nobel Prize in Physiology and Medical Science.

Problems can engage curiosity, inquiry and thinking in meaningful and powerful ways. Education needs a new perspective of searching for problems and looking at problems.

A story was told about a group of researchers working in a cornfield near Cornell University. It was a genetic experiment about the sterility of pollen from corn. The researchers observed discrepancies from what was expected, but most did not bother. A lady amongst them named Barbara McClintock decided to take ownership of the problem. In those days very few people were interested in the study of chromosomes, their genetic content and expressions (what is known today as cytogenetics). Decades later McClintock said: "When you suddenly see the problem, something happens." Her immersion in the problem led to an insight about mobile genetic elements – a discovery that is recognized today as the bedrock of life sciences. The story took place in the 1930s and McClintock was awarded the Nobel Prize in 1983.

In education, we need to learn more from the legacy of scientific discoveries. The ability to see a problem from a mass of information, learning to make observations and connections, and the attitude of taking ownership of problems are important aspects of learning and thinking.

Sometimes immersion in a problem leads to spin-off discoveries. At a Stanford alumni gathering in Singapore, Professor Douglas Osheroff shared with us how his work led to the discovery that won the Nobel Prize. Osheroff was then a graduate student of David Lee and Robert Richardson at Cornell University. At that time they were looking for "a phase transition to a kind of magnetic order in frozen helium-3 ice", but being immersed in the problem resulted in his observation and insight that brought about the discovery of a different phenomenon: the superfluidity of helium-3. The breakthrough in low-temperature physics won the team the 1996 Nobel Prize in Physics.

Think of the Japanese engineer who, whilst taking a walk in the park, contemplated how one could combine outdoor exercise, enjoyment of music and appreciation of nature all at the same time. His preoccupation with this problem led to the invention of tiny stereo and headphones – the Walkman.

When working as a consultant with Philips Electronics on enhancing the innovativeness of one of its most successful division –

development of domestic appliances – I had the opportunity to interact with many scientists and engineers working on a variety of pre-development ideas and projects. When I spoke to their most innovative people (based on data provided by their management staff on who were some of their most inventive personnel), I found that their engagement with problems was somewhat different from that of the average research engineer. They demonstrated a special motivation, holistic involvement and abilities to harness resources and intelligences. They knew how to generate ideas, to be divergent in their thinking and at the same time be analytical and systematic. They used analogical thinking, saw the big picture and were able to bring ideas into fruition. They knew what to connect to and when and how to connect. They also did not work in isolation; they knew how to collaborate.

The challenge for education is to develop the kinds of thinking skills I have just described. Multinational corporations and organizations are seeking people with such competencies. According to International Business Machines (IBM), the people they hire must possess the following com-petencies: problem-solving ability, teamwork spirit, interpersonal skills, creativity, project management skills and a systems perspective.

Breakthroughs in science and technology are often the result of fascination with problems. Great learning often begins with preoccupation with a problem, followed by taking ownership of the problem and harnessing of multiple dimensions of thinking.

Problems and Pedagogy

It is not difficult to imagine that in the life science class described earlier, instead of posing a problem scenario, the teacher simply presents some facts of biology or chemistry on the topic. The opportunities to stimulate curiosity, inquiry, engagement and motivation in learning would be drastically reduced if not lost. We may not necessarily be teaching the brightest cohort of students. We are not talking about producing top-league Nobel Prize–winning scientists either. The examples cited earlier are meant to illustrate

Problems and the questions associated with them when strategically posed can enhance the depth and quality of thinking. What is often lacking in edu-cation today is the effective use of inquiry and problem-based learning approaches.

and to inspire us to take a fresh look at problems. In the ordinary classroom, the value of using problems to stimulate learning can never be overemphasized.

Many education systems are characterized by a structure of learning as shown in Figure 2.1. Learning in schools and even universities can be characterized as:

- learning by memorization
- learning by imitation
- learning by modelling

Learning by memorization begins in preschool and continues all the way to college education with a prevalence of information accumulation and knowledge recall. The predominance of paper-and-pencil testing and examinations also contributed to this mode of learning.

The kinds of so-called "problems" that students solve in many of our classes are actually exercises rather than problems. Teachers typically present in class a large number of examples accompanied by comprehensive guidelines and step-by-step solutions. Students are then given similar exercises of a variety of challenges. Often there is very little element of novelty, although these "problems" may call for synthesis and application of the knowledge learnt.

There is nothing wrong with such an approach as we need such a structured and organized approach for acquiring fundamental knowledge and foundations. These are important in establishing basic axioms, definitions and principles, particularly in disciplines like mathematics, language or basic sciences. There is, however, an overdependence on learning through worked examples and routine exercises. As a result, there is very limited use of the power of problems.

One should note that when to pose a problem and what should be the scope of the problem have in the past been limited by the learner's lack of accessibility to information. The Internet revolution has

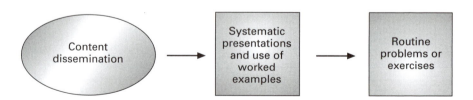

Figure 2.1 Representation of a typical structure of learning in the traditional education system

redefined the role of educators and ushered in new possibilities in the use of problems.

For simplicity, we may classify the types of problems along a continuum of routine versus novel and artificiality versus the real world as shown in Figure 2.2. Most problems in schools would be categorized into the lower left quadrant. These routine–artificial problems are your homework exercises and examination-type questions. Sometimes we have more challenge and complexity in these artificial problems, which could be referred to as puzzles.

Lee Shulman (1991) observed that Jerome Bruner in his essay "The Art of Discovery" cited an English philosopher Weldon who used an aphorism about three kinds of challenges in this world. They are troubles, puzzles and problems:

- Troubles are unformed, inchoate, and terribly hard to focus and manage.
- Puzzles are well structured, neat and artificial.
- When you have a puzzle to place on your trouble, that is when you have a problem to work on.

According to Professor Shulman (1991) of Stanford:

> *Education is a process of helping people develop capacities to learn how to connect their troubles with useful puzzles to form problems. Educators fail most miserably when they fail to see that the only justification for learning to do puzzles is when they relate to troubles. When the puzzles take on a life of their own – problem sets employing mindless algorithms, lists of names . . . definitions – they cease to represent education. The puzzles become disconnected from troubles and remain mere puzzles. We may refer to them as problems, but that is a form of word magic, for they are not real problems (p. 2).*

What Weldon, Bruner and Shulman alluded to as troubles are what we refer to as real-world problems. Problem-based learning (PBL) is about learning to solve problems in the novel–real world quadrant in Figure 2.2.

Problems and Multiple Perspectives

We mentioned earlier that we are not discounting learning by memorization and imitation. Similarly, learning by modelling has its merits. Indeed, the human brain and its memory system have much to gain from such systematic learning.

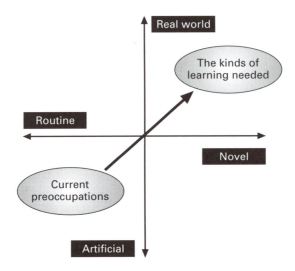

Figure 2.2 Types of problems in curricula

In many education systems, students somehow develop a tendency to think that there is a single correct answer to any one problem. In fact, Evans and colleagues (2002) found that people have a tendency to focus on a single hypothesis in problem-solving situations. In the classroom, learning by modelling often brings with it an overreliance on so-called experts. Whilst we need to model from certain expertise, what is often missing is the creative use of real-world problems. The way modelling is done often results in rather narrow, compartmentalized and inflexible systems of thinking. This problem is accentuated by the tendency towards episodic and narrow perspectives as well as unwarranted constraints of worldviews.

In Chapter 1, we reflected on the changes around us. The problems confronting the world and individuals will come with increasing rapidity, complexity and diversity. Corollaries include:

> **In solving real-world problems, we need to realize that a whole range of cognitive processes and mental activities are involved. The mind has to go through cycles and iterations of systematic, systemic, generative, analytical and divergent thinking.**

- problems of increasing quantity and difficulty
- newer problems and shorter time frame for solutions
- more global (larger-scale) problems requiring integrated solutions

Following the Industrial Revolution, for a variety of reasons, specialization was developed to expedite the solution of problems. The socioeconomic developments also required education to accelerate the process of producing experts in specialized fields.

The 21st century, however, will be characterized by enhanced connectivity. This means that reality cannot be easily divided. Real-world issues are cross-disciplinary and involve multiple perspectives. We will need a helicopter view of things and the synthesis of a diversity of interrelated knowledge bases.

Learning Theories, Constructivism and PBL

As the National Research Council (1999) of the US National Academy of Sciences noted: "The quest to understand human learning has, in the past four decades, undergone dramatic change. Once a matter for philosophical argument, the workings of the mind and brain are now subject to powerful research tools. From that research, a science of learning is emerging" (p. 5). Research on memory and knowledge, for example, points to the importance of memory not only as associations but more importantly as connections and meaningful coherent structures. We now know more about "novice" learners and "expert" learners. We can develop better learning in individuals by providing opportunities for acquisition of procedures and skills through dealing with information in a problem space and learning of general strategies of problem solving. Instead of traditional schooling, we may need to look at new ways of engaging the individual, taking into account "plasticity of development" as well as cultural, community and social environmental contexts. The report also highlighted that apart from emphasizing behaviours and performance there is a need to realize that individuals can be taught metacognitive processes and self-regulatory thinking.

From the pedagogical perspective, PBL is based on the constructivist theory of learning (Schmidt, 1993; Savery & Duffy, 1995; Hendry & Murphy, 1995). In PBL approaches:

- understanding is derived from interaction with the problem scenario and the learning environment
- engagement with the problem and the problem inquiry process creates cognitive dissonance that stimulates learning
- knowledge evolves through collaborative processes of social negotiation and evaluation of the viability of one's point of view

The underpinning philosophy of constructivism in PBL is not new. Four decades ago the well-known philosopher of education John

Dewey (1963) wrote:

> *There is, I think, no point in the philosophy of progressive education which is sounder than its emphasis upon the importance of the participation of the learner in the formation of the purposes which direct his activities in the learning process, just as there is no defect in traditional education greater than its failure to secure the active cooperation of pupil in construction of the purposes involved in the studying (p. 63).*

Constructivism has been repeatedly emphasized (e.g. Biggs, 1996; Carlson, 1999), yet in teacher training and in our classroom the reality is often one of didactic teaching with little room for dynamic thinking and dialogue.

PBL in the classroom is not only about infusing problems into the class but also about creating opportunities for students to construct knowledge through effective interactions and collaborative inquiry.

Karl Popper (1992), the famous philosopher of science whose ideas also influenced education, once wrote:

> *I dreamt of one day founding a school in which young people could learn without boredom, and would be stimulated to pose problems and discuss them; a school in which no unwanted answers to unasked questions would have to be listened to; in which one did not study for the sake of passing examinations (p. 40).*

Perhaps a PBL school could be an answer to Popper's dream. In PBL, learners are given the opportunity to find knowledge for themselves and to deliberate with others. They then refine and restructure their own knowledge in the light of prior and new knowledge and experiences. Through self-directed learning, peer learning, team teaching and presentation activities, the cognitive processes are thus enriched.

Developments in cognitive science and neuroscience also support the use of problems in learning. Seeing configurations (the whole is more than the sum of its parts), understanding perceptions, cognitive dissonance, problem solving and insightful learning are important aspects of learning in cognitive psychology. For example, as educators, we are familiar with the use of learning objectives. We organize our lectures and lessons sequentially and systematically with clear and specific learning objectives along each stage. Whilst these may be important in teaching basic facts and establishing foundation knowledge, they are not as effective with developing higher-order thinking skills. The development of insightful and creative thinking does not happen this way. On the contrary, when people are immersed in solving a problem over an extended period of time, they often derive insights and "aha" revelations not in ways in which we sequence learning objectives. There are many aspects of learning, and thinking could perhaps be best developed through immersion in a problem scenario. These aspects may include cognitive functions such as the following:

- Configuring (systems and holistic thinking)
- Relearning
- Rethinking
- Observing and making use of observations
- Recognizing and making patterns
- Generating fresh arguments and explanations
- Analogizing
- Connecting
- Imaging
- Abstracting
- Empathizing
- Transforming information
- Playing with ideas

This list is not meant to be exhaustive or systematic in any way. It merely serves to point out that there are many aspects of good thinking and learning that we need to address in a more innovative education system. Figure 2.3 shows the shift needed in addressing our pedagogical paradigms.

Figure 2.4 provides a schema of PBL approaches where problems trigger learning by inquiry, which results in learning to deal with more novel and real-world problems.

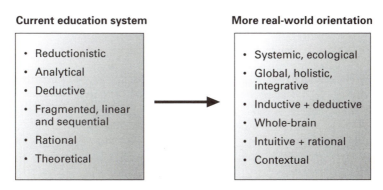

Figure 2.3 A paradigm shift for education systems

PBL and Cognition

Jerome Bruner, at one time Director of the Harvard Center for Cognitive Studies, wrote a famous classic entitled *The Process of Education*. In it Bruner (1960) argued that the knowledgeable person is a problem solver, one who interacts with the environment in testing hypotheses, developing generalizations and engaging in learning to arrive at solutions. According to Bruner, the goal of education is to further the development of problem-solving skills and the process of inquiry and discussion. As Jim Killian, former president of the Massachusetts Institute of Technology put it: "The basic aim of education is not to accumulate knowledge, but rather to learn to think creatively, teach oneself and seek answers to questions as yet unexplored."

From the cognitive perspective, all problems have three elements (Mayer, 1983; Chi & Glaser, 1985):

- An initial state (problem situation)
- A goal state (problem resolution)
- Process and means to get from initial state to goal state

In many PBL approaches, the student confronts a situation where he or she needs to accomplish an objective, and the means (i.e. the information, process and actions to be taken) is something new or unknown to the student. In many ways, the pedagogy of PBL helps to make "visible" or explicit the thinking and the richness of the cognitive structuring and processes involved.

Figure 2.5 illustrates how PBL problems affect cognition and learning. A problem triggers the context for engagement, curiosity, inquiry and a quest to address real-world issues. What goes on in the mind of the learner (cognition) and the probable changes in behaviour (learning) include those listed in the right-hand box of the figure.

The challenge in diversifying educational methods is designing learning through the effective use of problems. Depending on the

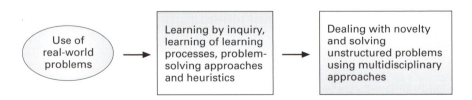

Figure 2.4 Schema of PBL approaches

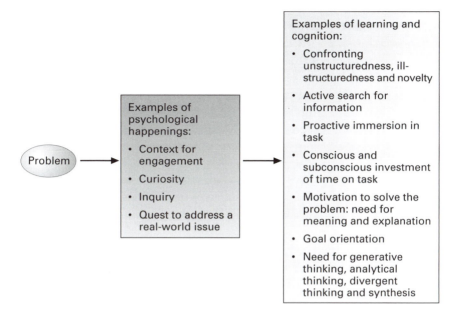

Figure 2.5 PBL and cognition

nature of the discipline, the goals of the curriculum, the flexibility of cross-disciplinary integration and the availability of resources (e.g. time, infrastructure, information systems), problems can be used appropriately, strategically and powerfully.

Problems can be used to challenge and empower students to capitalize on the accessibility to and the wealth of knowledge

> **PBL optimizes on goals, needs and the motivation that drives learning. It simulates the kind of problem-solving cognition needed in real-world challenges. The PBL innovation incorporates the use of e-learning accessibility, creative interdisciplinary pursuits and the development of people skills.**

today. Furthermore, the knowledge fields of this century will increasingly be characterized by the creative integration of knowledge from diverse disciplines. Biotechnology, the life sciences, telecommunications, material science and supercomputers are examples of corollaries of effective multidisciplinary pursuits. Many of these pursuits originated from intense curiosity and the motivation to solve real-world problems. The use of PBL approaches aims to enhance such knowledge sharing and enterprise.

3

WHAT IS PROBLEM-BASED LEARNING?

PBL in Professional Training

In their attempts to innovate learning, educators are exploring methodologies that emphasize these facets:

- Real-world challenges
- Higher-order thinking skills
- Problem-solving skills
- Interdisciplinary learning
- Independent learning
- Information-mining skills
- Teamwork
- Communication skills

PBL approaches appear to be promising in addressing most of these needs. More importantly, PBL is able to address these holistically.

PBL is by no means new. Medical colleges such as Case Western Reserve Medical School, McMaster University Medical School and the University of New Mexico Medical School explored the use of PBL as early as the 1950s. In the 1980s the consortium of medical schools in the United States, which comprises leading medical schools such as Cornell, Duke, Harvard, Johns Hopkins, Pittsburg, Stanford, Washington and Yale, was often concerned with the challenge of how to produce first-rate medical practitioners. Cuban (1999), for example, noted that the desired qualities of medical practitioners included competencies and attitudes pertaining to medical proficiency, humaneness, public service, staying abreast of new knowledge, and scientific inquiry. Communication of one's beliefs, values, knowledge and skills through coaching, advising and research was also an essential practice. There was recognition that a good medical education would include a core of essential medical knowledge and learning the "problems of medicine" rather than just acquisition of techniques and accumulation of data. It was also recommended that there should be as little separation as possible between preclinical and clinical work and that integrated teaching would be preferred. In 1988 the Harvard University Medical School adopted New Pathways, a PBL programme for all its students (Cuban, 1999).

Medical education is one of the most expensive investments anywhere in the world. Effective preparation and development of medical and health professionals is of great importance for obvious reasons. Given the immensity and rapid development of medical information and knowledge, the need for quick decision making, reasoning and problem solving, and the need to work with limited resources under constraints of short-handedness, urgency and crisis, learning has really got to be effective. Professional education and education in general can learn much from the developments in medical training (Vernon & Blake, 1993; Norman & Schmidt, 2000).

Why has PBL proliferated in medical education? Bridges and Hallinger (1995) noted that one of the arguments for the use of PBL in medical education was that empirical evidence showed medical students retaining little of what they had learnt in the basic disciplines. Furthermore, studies such as those by Balla (1990a, b) found that medical students often applied basic science knowledge incorrectly or not at all in formulating and revising clinical diagnoses. Traditionally, content knowledge is taught separately from practice to students in lectures. It has been argued that this passive accumulation of knowledge (which is detached from the real-world context) does not help learners apply knowledge to novel problem situations. PBL appears to address this gap between theory and practice. Barrows and Tamblyn (1980) observed that PBL is "learning that results from the process of working toward the understanding or resolution of a problem" (p. 18).

Norman and Schmidt (1992) wrote that there is evidence to suggest that PBL enhances:

- transfer of concepts to new problems
- integration of concepts
- intrinsic interest in learning
- self-directed learning
- learning skills

Meta-analysis of literature on PBL in medical education by Albanese and Mitchell (1993) revealed that PBL helps students in the construction of knowledge and reasoning skills compared with the traditional teaching approach. PBL is now used in most of the medical schools in the United States (Bridges & Hallinger, 1995) and in Australia (Hendry & Murphy, 1995). Many medical and health science programmes in the United Kingdom and Asia Pacific (e.g. University of Hong Kong and National University of Singapore) have also adopted PBL.

Historically, several technological universities in Europe with strong links to industry have actually adopted PBL approaches without explicitly emphasizing the approach. Aalborg University in Denmark, for example, has a tradition of asking corporations and industry to provide its postgraduate students with problems that the companies are working on or cannot solve. Problems become the starting point of the engineering curricula. The University of Maastricht in the Netherlands similarly employs the use of problems in their business and medical curricula.

Many postgraduate executive business training programmes are in essence problem-based. The programmes of institutions like Stanford University, Harvard University and INSEAD employ a prolific use of real-world problem cases as starting points and anchors for the learning of business-related disciplines. PBL, however, should not be confused with case-study approaches. In PBL, the problem rather than content knowledge is always presented first. Problems are the motivation for learning.

PBL in Education

Whilst PBL is not a new philosophy or approach to learning, it has now become an educational innovation owing to several recent developments, such as the Internet revolution and breakthroughs in multidisciplinary pursuits. Interest in PBL has also gained momentum across various disciplines, such as engineering, architecture and business (Tan et al., 2000; Savin-Baden, 2000; Little et al., 2001).

In the 1990s many high schools, junior high schools and elementary schools in the United States began to introduce PBL into their curricula. Studies such as that by Achilles and Hoover (1996) support the use of PBL as a vehicle for school improvement.

According to Robert Delisle (1997, 7):

Problem-based learning (PBL) works well with all students, making its strategies ideal for heterogeneous classrooms where students with mixed abilities can pool their talents collaboratively to invent a solution. These techniques also lend themselves to an interdisciplinary orientation since answering a problem frequently requires information from several academic areas... Teachers... say they have seen their students learn more material, understand more ideas, and enjoy school more.

West (1992) found that at the secondary school level PBL was effective in stimulating interest in science, enhancing knowledge construction and improving problem-solving skills. Trop and Sage (1998) advocated the use of PBL across kindergarten through grade 12 (K–12). There are now a huge number of Web sites on the use of PBL in US schools (see the Appendix for recommended sites). For example, the Web site of the Center for Problem-based Learning of the Illinois Mathematics and Science Academy (IMSA) (www.imsa.edu) provides several good examples of problems for the K–12 levels. One can also find Web sites on the use of PBL with primary-age children, such as the Jerome School District in the state of Idaho.

Impetus for the use of PBL includes its sound philosophy in the light of pedagogical and real-world developments (as discussed in the earlier chapters). Commonly cited reasons for using PBL in US schools include the value of:

- using real-life issues
- active engagement
- interdisciplinary learning
- student making choices in learning
- collaborative learning

It is also argued that PBL helps raise the quality of education through its emphasis on problem solving and thinking.

Nature and Characteristics of PBL Approaches

PBL approaches in a curriculum usually include the following characteristics (Tan, 2002c):

- The problem is the *starting point* of learning.
- The problem is usually a *real-world* problem that appears unstructured. If it is a simulated problem, it is meant to be as authentic as possible.

- The problem calls for *multiple perspectives*. The use of cross-disciplinary knowledge is a key feature in many PBL curricula. In any case, PBL encourages the solution of the problem by taking into consideration knowledge from various subjects and topics.
- The problem challenges students' current knowledge, attitudes and competencies, thus calling for identification of learning needs and *new areas of learning*.
- *Self-directed learning* is primary. Thus, students assume major responsibility for the acquisition of information and knowledge.
- *Harnessing of a variety of knowledge sources* and the use and evaluation of information resources are essential PBL processes.
- Learning is *collaborative, communicative and cooperative*. Students work in small groups with a high level of interaction for peer learning, peer teaching and group presentations.
- Development of *inquiry and problem-solving skills* is as important as content knowledge acquisition for the solution of the problem. The PBL tutor thus facilitates and coaches through questioning and cognitive coaching.
- Closure in the PBL process includes *synthesis and integration* of learning.
- PBL also concludes with an *evaluation and review* of the learner's experience and the learning processes.

The goals of PBL thus include content learning, acquisition of process skills and problem-solving skills, and lifewide learning. I would like to introduce the term *lifewide learning* to emphasize skills such as self-directed learning, independent information mining, collaborative learning and reflective thinking. Others have used the term *lifelong learning*, which is entirely appropriate as it emphasizes the need for continuous learning and the timeless nature of learning. Since most educators are dealing primarily with young people (secondary and university students), who appear not too concerned about the longevity of their learning, I decided to use a somewhat different term here! In any case, the point about lifewide learning is that through PBL students acquire

> **The goals of PBL are content learning, acquisition of discipline-related heuristics and development of problem-solving skills. PBL also includes the lifewide learning goals of self-directed learning, information-mining skills, collaborative and team learning, and reflective and evaluative thinking skills.**

competencies that can be transferred across various life and work situations. The skills learnt are applicable to learning in a new discipline or learning to do something new.

A PBL Case Study

Figure 3.1 illustrates the key components in PBL approaches, which will be considered in detail next using a case study.

Problem Presentation

We shall consider a simple PBL example in economics to illustrate these components and their characteristics. One of the typical topics in economics concerns the various types of business units. Students may be expected to explain the purposes and characteristics of units such as sole proprietorships, partnerships, private limited companies and public listed companies. Traditionally, a teacher would give a series of lectures beginning with one on sole proprietorship and moving on sequentially to the other types of registered businesses. However, a lecturer may choose to use a PBL approach by posing the following problem:

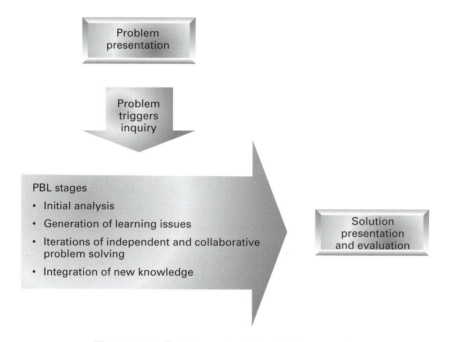

Figure 3.1 Components of the PBL approach

You and two of your friends would like to start a business to design
Web pages for corporate clients. Amongst you there is a great deal
of expertise in Web-based programming. Each of you agreed to put
in $2,000 to start this business. How would you go about registering
and setting up your business?

Problem Triggers Inquiry

Thus, instead of having a didactic delivery and students passively
copying notes, students are now presented with a real-world problem
scenario as the starting point of learning. Learning thus begins with
meeting a somewhat messy and unstructured problem. The problem
triggers learning by having students:

- define the problem
- analyse the problem
- generate ideas (and hypotheses)
- identify learning issues

Students are usually given sufficient time to study the problem
individually before they are formed into groups. They are encouraged
to underline key words and jot down ideas and questions that come to
their minds.

PBL Stages: Initial Analysis and Generation of Learning Issues

Students work in small groups (of 3–4 people) to discuss the problem
scenario. They ask themselves questions, such as what they know from
the problem presented, what they need to know and what ideas come
to mind. They are expected to paraphrase the problem and come up
with a problem statement to describe the scope of their engagement.
Many questions will arise. In this case, some of the questions raised
may be:

- What is the goal of our company?
- What must we know about the different kinds of business
  units?
- Should it be a partnership or limited company?
- What are the legal requirements?
- How do we go about registering the business?

Hence, instead of being told what a partnership or limited company is
and being presented with the sequence of planning and registering a

business, the students now need to inquire, seek information from books and Web sites, and think about how to solve the problem. Apart from the economics perspective pertaining to types of business units, they also need to consider other perspectives, such as the legal aspects of registering a business and accounting requirements.

As the students deliberate on the problem, brainstorming and discussing collaboratively, they are expected to draw up their learning issues and objectives based on the questions raised. They then divide the work amongst themselves to seek the necessary information on their own. In a group discussion facilitated by their PBL tutor, the students refine their learning objectives into more pertinent questions that require the acquisition of deeper knowledge and insights important for their future professional practice. In this case, their learning issues and objectives may be stated in the form of questions such as the following:

- What are the various types of business units?
- What are the types of business units appropriate for the given purpose of the business?
- What are the advantages and disadvantages of a partnership versus a private limited company?
- What are the legal requirements associated with the registration of the business?

PBL Stages: Iterations of Independent and Collaborative Problem Solving, Integration of New Knowledge, Presentation and Evaluation

The questions raised provide the parameters and motivation for learning. The learning objectives are attained through self-directed learning and group discussions mediated by the tutor. Several meeting and learning sessions may follow depending on the structure of the PBL process. In a PBL course that I know, students were actually made to present a business proposal with actual forms from the registry of businesses and companies duly completed and submitted to the tutor. In the process, the students actively sought information about liabilities, tax policies and the advantages of the various types of businesses. They also went through the planning processes through active discussion and even interviewed people who were running businesses of their own.

At the closure, students contextualize and integrate their learning from presentations made by team members and peer groups. The tutor facilitates synthesis of the new knowledge and competencies acquired. The concluding session would also incorporate the students' reflection, review and evaluation of various aspects of the learning.

Schema of the PBL Process

Figure 3.2 provides a schema of a typical PBL process (Tan, 2002c). Each stage of the process will be elaborated next.

Meeting the Problem

At this stage, the problem scenario acts as a stimulus to scaffold and extend a realistic context students might encounter in the future. The activities in this first tutorial include:

- developing collegiality
- individual reading, reflection and inquiry

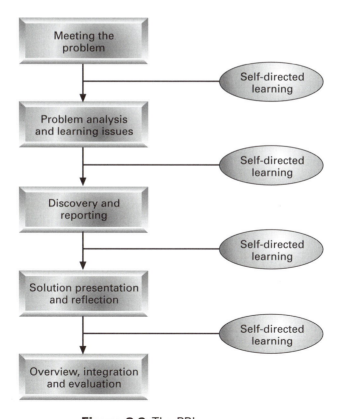

Figure 3.2 The PBL process

- commitment to team roles and to the group
- brainstorming and articulation of probable issues
- consensus on problem statement
- commitment to deliberate on problem scenario and problem analysis

Problem Analysis and Learning Issues

What follows is an induction into self-directed learning. At this stage, the students' prior knowledge is activated and ideas are generated that call for further learning. Students are required to work independently on their own, searching for information through various resources. This tutorial thus involves:

- brainstorming and analysis of problem (e.g. generation of possible explanations and hypotheses)
- identification of learning issues and formulation of learning objectives
- assignment of self-directed learning and peer teaching

Here the tutor emphasizes the idea that real-life issues are often fuzzy and, faced with problems, we need to seek theories and sometimes multidisciplinary knowledge bases to address the various issues we have to tackle. The groups then proceed to make a list of issues amongst themselves and agree to seek information from books, journals, Internet resources and so on and to come back with better-informed explanations to the issues and questions posed.

Discovery and Reporting

Following the research and self-directed learning, students report their discovery of learning to their own groups. At this peer-teaching stage, students gather to share the new information they have individually discovered.

Students practise group collaboration and communication skills through questions and the seeking of further information from one another. The PBL tutor helps ensure that key areas to be learnt are not overlooked and also quizzes students on the accuracy, reliability and validity of the information obtained.

Solution Presentation and Reflection

An iterative process follows with the discovery of learning, reporting, peer teaching and presentation of solutions. When students present their solutions to the problem scenario, a reflective and evaluative approach is taken. This involves contextualization and application of the knowledge to the situation. Students rephrase and paraphrase the knowledge acquired and demonstrate their new knowledge. Sometimes more questions may be asked. The tutor helps students to clarify doubts, to beware of gaps and to correct misconceptions or over-generalizations.

Overview, Integration and Evaluation

The integration of knowledge from various disciplines and sources and the synthesis of ideas shared bring the PBL process to closure. The review and evaluation of learning, however, forms an integral part of learning. Students are encouraged to critique their learning resources (their value, reliability and usefulness for future learning). They reflect on the new knowledge they have learnt as a result of the problem. The tutor helps summarize and integrate major principles and concepts at this stage. Group members also evaluate how they do as learners in terms of being a problem solver, a self-directed learner and as members of the team.

Variations in PBL Approaches

The PBL process described in the schema of Figure 3.2 could be part of a curriculum that takes about six weeks with one session each week. Following the formal PBL tutorials and meeting sessions, time is needed for self-directed learning. If the problem is more complex, it may take a longer period with more iterations of "problem analysis and learning issues" and "discovery and reporting" before the groups move on to the "solution presentation" phase.

Many variations are possible in the design of PBL activities depending on the purpose and goals of the curriculum. For example, Tan (2000d) modified the PBL activities of IMSA that were developed by Trop and Sage (1998) to emphasize cognitive and metacognitive learning as the "content" of learning using adventure and experiential problems. The model is as shown in Figure 3.3. In this case, the participants were immersed in an intensive one-day learning and there was less time devoted to self-directed information mining.

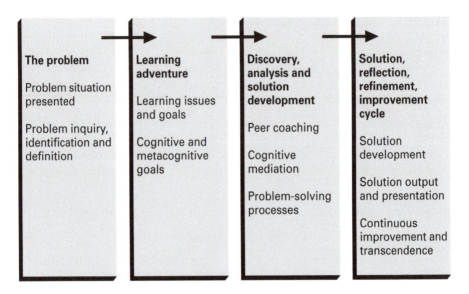

Figure 3.3 One-time intensive PBL immersion

The type of PBL and model adopted can vary depending on the relative emphasis of the following goals:

- Acquisition of multidisciplinary content knowledge
- Acquisition of process skills and heuristics of the disciplines
- Learning of problem-solving skills
- Learning of collaborative skills
- Learning of lifewide skills

A problem could be on a particular topic, such as one specific to science:

You are joining a humanitarian mission that will be involved in erecting the building for an orphanage. Owing to the extremely hot summer and cold winter, it is important to take note of ways to maintain temperatures in the building. You have been tasked to be the "heat" consultant.

The scope of the problem could be delimited to the study of heat transfer. The problem could involve activation of prior knowledge and search for information related to heat transfer of building materials and heat flow in open and closed spaces.

On the other hand, the problem could be expanded to include a building plan and the need to optimize the use of materials and so on to accommodate a given budget. It could then involve some mathematics. The problem may also include a study of the geography of a particular city in Mongolia where knowledge of climatic conditions, location of and accessibility to transportation and so on is needed.

Figure 3.4 illustrates the various possibilities of learning that could be incorporated and emphasized through the problem. Students may also be expected to write and present their reports, in which case their language and writing skills would also be incorporated. Apart from expanding the multiple disciplines, the goals of the PBL module might include emphasis on teamwork and presentation skills.

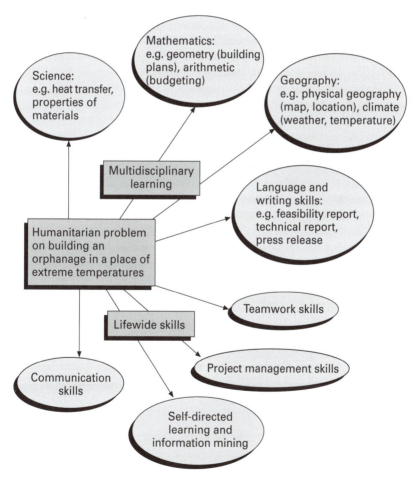

Figure 3.4 Example of possibilities and scope of learning

Problem Complexity and Goals

The nature and scope of the problems and the PBL cycle to be adopted will depend on the goals of using PBL. Many innovations are thus possible. When the goals of using PBL are broader and more multifaceted, the problem may be more complex and a longer PBL cycle may be required.

Figure 3.5 depicts the types of problems that could be presented in PBL, while Figure 3.6 shows the extent of lifewide skills to be incorporated as a continuum. Some PBL modules are designed primarily to emphasize skills such as information mining and collaboration; as such the nature of the problem presented and the learning environment designed will be very different.

The kind of PBL to be infused into the curriculum also depends on the profile and maturity of the students and their previous experiences, the flexibility of the existing curriculum, assessment expectations, and the time and resources available. The lifewide goals of the PBL module will have implications on the degree of facilitation, mediation and scaffolding needed.

As observed by Barrows (1986), there are many possible combinations of design variables in PBL approaches. There can also be a combination of teaching approaches with PBL. For example, Armstrong (1991) noted that a hybrid model was practised in Harvard Medical School where PBL, lectures, laboratory sessions and other teaching strategies are incorporated in the curriculum.

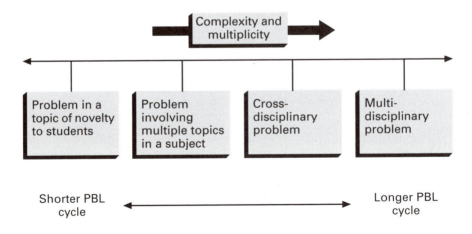

Figure 3.5 Problem complexity and multiplicity

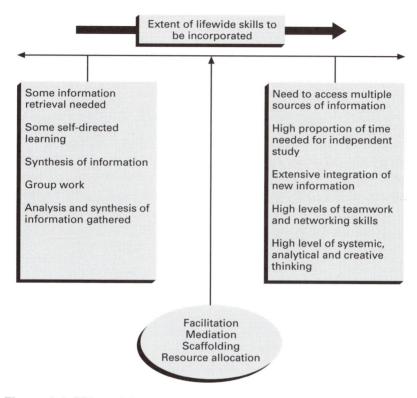

Figure 3.6 PBL goals in terms of the extent of lifewide skills to be learnt

In short, PBL involves using real-world problems to trigger learning and optimizing on the power of problems to incorporate key learning processes. The design of PBL will depend on the goals and outcomes that we wish to accomplish to impact on learning.

4

FACILITATING PROBLEM-BASED LEARNING PROCESSES

Teachers' Roles in PBL

In a knowledge-based economy, we need new responses in the way we deal with knowledge and learners' participation. Teachers and students alike are confronted with the need to reexamine their views of:

- knowledge
- teacher–student interactions
- peer interactions
- interactions with the information milieu

Derek Bok, a former president of Harvard University, noted his observation of instruction in schools (1993, 179):

The bulk of instructional time finds students listening to teachers talk, working on tasks that require little application of concepts, imagination, or serious inquiry. Description after description documents the Sahara of instruction demanding little thought from students.

Twenty-five years ago, Professor Arnold Arons (1978) at the University of Washington wrote: "Experience makes it increasingly clear that purely verbal presentations – lecturing at large groups of students who passively expect to absorb ideas that actually demand intense deductive and inductive mental activity coupled with personal observation and experience – leave virtually nothing permanent or significant in the student mind" (p. 105).

Student learning is a major focus of educational institutions. In what ways are students learning? In what directions are teachers directing their energies? What are institutions doing to make education relevant and to add value to the education process?

In Chapter 1, I talked about a shift in curriculum pertaining to three foci of preoccupation. This is represented in Figure 4.1. The teacher's role in PBL is very different from that in a didactic classroom. In PBL, the teacher thinks in terms of the following:

> **We need to use learning processes that will move students towards independent, lifewide and lifelong learning. The learning environments we establish should encourage reflective thinking, critical evaluation and inventive thinking.**

- How can I design and use real-world problems (rather than what content to disseminate) as anchors around which students could achieve the learning outcomes?
- How do I coach students in problem-solving processes, self-direction and peer learning (instead of how best to teach and give information)?
- How will students see themselves as active problem solvers (rather than passive listeners)?

Likewise, in PBL the teacher focuses on:

- facilitating the PBL processes of learning (e.g. changing mindsets, developing inquiry skills, engaging in collaborative learning)
- coaching students in the heuristics (strategies) of problem solving (e.g. deep reasoning, metacognition, critical thinking, systems thinking)

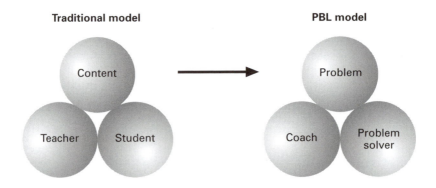

Figure 4.1 Shift in the three foci of preoccupation

- mediating the process of acquiring information (e.g. scanning the information environment, accessing multiple information sources, making connections)

Figure 4.2 illustrates these roles of the teacher in PBL and Figure 4.3 shows the teacher's role as a designer of the learning environment through the use of problems. In fulfilling these roles, the teacher manages the learning process and provides the necessary interventions to ensure that students acquire relevant knowledge and higher-order

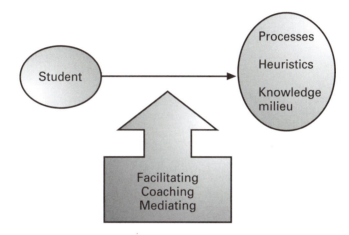

Figure 4.2 The roles of teacher in PBL

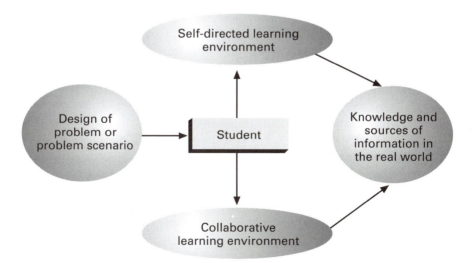

Figure 4.3 Design of the learning environment

thinking skills (reasoning, heuristics and metacognitive skills). The teacher also facilitates, coaches and mediates so that students acquire competencies to become independent, self-directed learners and learn to communicate and socialize effectively as team members.

To be effective facilitators, we have first got to change our own mindsets about learning. As Professor Arons (1978) argued:

> *If we are serious about cultivating some measure of the kind of understanding I have been defining . . . we must give students time to learn; the pace must be slow enough to let them confront evidence, to think and contemplate, to relive some of the steps by which the human mind first achieved these insights. This means we must cut down on "coverage." It is futile and fatuous to drown students in a stream of names and jargon (p. 110).*

More recently, Larry Cuban (1999), when referring to arguments about enhancing medical education, cited:

> *Faculty wanted students to have "more time for reflection, for unhurried contemplative reading, for assimilating the best of the original literature in each field." They wanted students to learn that "real study is more rewarding than cramming," and that "all our present knowledge serves mainly as a springboard into the fascinating unknown" (p. 147).*

In today's fast-paced world where the half-life of knowledge is shortened, it is even more important for us to have the mindset that depth, imagination and insights and the processes of learning in a discipline are more important than the mere coverage of content. Many teachers, however, are used to teaching and disseminating content only. Owing to the examination system, we also tend to adopt a "just-in-case" attitude and cover more and more content. This is contrary to what is needed in the real world today: "just-in-time" knowledge.

Preparing Students' Mindsets

It is not easy for students to shift their mindset from one of spoon-feeding to one of inquiry and self-directed learning. Before implementing PBL, it is useful to prepare students, especially when PBL is going to feature as a major part of the curriculum.

Students are easily locked into narrow perceptions and tend to do only what is required to clear the immediate academic hurdle. It is a tragedy of the education system if students only want to know how and not why. Some form of orientation and induction is needed to help students get an idea of the processes and the "end in mind". Help them to realize that the challenges of the world and expectations of higher education and employers are very different today. Explain why their education needs to be aligned with emphasis on skills such as (1) learning how to learn (self-directed, independent learning), (2) acquiring of depth of content and professional knowledge, (3) working collaboratively, (4) employing interdisciplinary knowledge, and (5) using critical inquiry and reflective practices.

The following are some important pointers to prepare students for PBL:

- Help students shift their mindset.
- Explain what PBL is in terms of what students might experience.
- Give students an overview of the PBL cycle, structure and time frame.
- Communicate the goals, outcomes and expectations.
- Prepare students for the novelty and the frustrations they may face.
- Help students take ownership of problems.

To reinforce the preparation of students for a major PBL curriculum, some of the information can be put succinctly into a handbook or on a Web site, which may include:

- Message from the professor or coordinator to encourage a positive attitude to change
- A statement about the real-world expectations of graduates or the kinds of professions students are being trained for
- A description of the curriculum and where PBL features in the curriculum
- The what, why and benefits of PBL
- Frequently asked questions
- Testimonies from previous PBL participants
- Employers' endorsement or testimonials of their employees who graduated from PBL courses

Emphasizing Collaborative Learning

PBL provides an excellent vehicle for collaborative inquiry and learning. Bray and his colleagues (2000) described collaborative inquiry as a process in which people are engaged in "repeated episodes of reflection and action" as they work in a group to "answer a question of importance to them" (p. 6). According to the authors, collaborative inquiry involves:

- formation of a collaborative inquiry group
- establishing conditions for group learning
- acting on inquiry questions
- making meaning by constructing knowledge

In PBL classes, learning is done in small groups. Small group learning provides opportunities for students to be actively involved and engaged in interactive inquiry and group learning, with the aim to:

- gain a deeper understanding of the knowledge (content and process) being acquired
- learn problem-solving processes
- learn to benefit from team perspectives
- develop interpersonal and communication skills
- learn to be effective team contributors

There are two strong arguments for collaborative learning:

- Collaboration as a competence
- Value of collaboration in higher cognitive and metacognitive processes

Collaboration as a competence includes inter- and intrapersonal skills and effective communication and social skills. The ability to work in teams and collaborate effectively is critical for all professionals today. Globalization calls for effective communication across cultures and we need to learn to work with others for mutual benefit and the achievement of goals. Moreover, with increasing complexity and specialization, we need to share and optimize on the various strengths of people in a group.

While visiting an international aircraft corporation in 1995, I observed that the executives and engineers there seemed to enjoy arguing and criticizing one another's ideas. I learnt later that they have the mindset that whenever they have an idea they want to know if it is good and viable, so they always welcome critiques and opinions. I was told that if you simply say "it's great" to their idea, they may actually be insulted. They may say to you: "Please critique to help me improve – I am sure you have some ideas of how this can be further improved!" Such a culture seems to create a resilient mindset. I noticed the same kind of behaviour when I attended an executive management programme taught by Stanford professors. My fellow participants were mostly senior executives in multinational corporations and self-made entrepreneurs. They were always eager to speak aloud their thoughts and ideas. One of them, a vice-president of a cruise company, told me that it is easier to make use of others to evaluate your ideas than to do it yourself because you would have already stretched your limits thinking about the problem and about new ways to improve on it.

In the PBL process, students learn that teamwork and collaboration are important for developing cognitive processes pertaining to scanning the environment, understanding the problem, gathering essential data and analysing data, and elaborating on solutions. Dialogue is essential to ensure that we are not locked into our own limited or prejudiced perspectives. It is important for developing critical thinking and reflection.

Small group teaching in PBL also helps to make students' thinking "visible" to tutors. In traditional teaching, the lecturers' job is to make their thinking visible to the students by being clear, systematic and organized. We have, however, neglected an equally important, if not more important, aspect of education, which is for students to make visible to us their thinking. Are they only able to regurgitate information or are they sufficiently analytical? Are they learning to connect information and ideas? Do they see things in systemic (big picture) and systematic ways? Through collaborative discussions, students learn to inquire and employ metacognitive processes.

> **People have different perspectives and views about a problem. We should learn to exchange views to gain a better understanding of a problem situation rather than assume a "correct" or "best" answer in one's own mind. Furthermore, when it comes to understanding the different perspectives of a problem, it can be said that none of us is as smart as all of us.**

Facilitating Small Group Learning in PBL

In your PBL class, particularly if it is a new class, develop an environment of learning, sharing, collegiality and professionalism through appropriate ice-breaking activities. Get to know the students and facilitate communication amongst them.

If your tutorial group is small enough, with one tutor to ten students or fewer, small group learning is a lot easier. Owing to budget constraints in many institutions, tutorial classes are getting larger in number. Whatever the numbers, there are innovative ways to encourage small group learning. You can establish a small group learning climate by having ground rules about group work. For example, in a typical PBL class of say 24 students, we can break students into eight groups of three. They would be told that whenever it is time for group work they would be expected to form into groups and assume certain group roles immediately. The roles appointed are as follows:

- Chairperson: to facilitate the discussion and ensure focus
- Recorder: to capture in writing key points discussed
- Reporter: to listen with a view to presenting a summary to the class

If there is a fourth person, he or she can be the timekeeper and vice-chairperson. All these roles should be rotated in each tutorial, and the tutor may observe, monitor and assess these roles. The main purpose of assigning roles, however, is to ensure that group activities are productive. Experience tells us that often group work may not be productive because people do not proactively assume roles and take up responsibilities. Even at the workplace, more often than not group discussions take place with no productive follow-up and actions. Often no one jots down the key points, and important ideas are not captured for future deliberations. Furthermore, when the time comes for sharing and presentation, there may be no volunteers. Groups also tend to stray in discussions – talking about many things except the problem! By having a chairperson to keep the discussion going and to keep members focused, time is more optimally used.

Although it is recommended that students work in groups of three or four, the tutor may also use a variety of cooperative learning techniques to combine these groups at various stages of the PBL cycle to synergize the combination of ideas, sharing of learning and the presentation of ideas. For example, groups may be asked to focus on different aspects of the problem or learning issues. In peer teaching and learning, it is also possible to get members of different groups working on similar learning issues to collaborate and to do joint teaching in two or three combined groups to their peers.

Table 4.1 provides a list of some general guiding points for group facilitation.

Table 4.1 Facilitating PBL groups

- If the problem is not given beforehand, give time for more thorough individual reading. Get students to think, reflect and make notes.
- Move around to monitor the quality of discussion. Prompt, question and ensure intended scope and preoccupation.
- To kick off the discussion, encourage every student to articulate his or her perception of the problem so that everyone arrives at a clearer mental representation of the problem scenario.
- Initial brainstorming may involve putting down words, phrases and ideas that come to mind with respect to the scenario.
- Remember that PBL involves a problem and the commitment of problem solvers; hence, developing ownership of and commitment to the problem is an important aspect of the first tutorial.
- Ask students to develop a problem statement for each problem scenario. The statement is an articulation of how the group paraphrases and takes ownership of the problem.
- Refrain from giving answers, disseminating or teaching anything (except PBL processes) in the first session!
- Ask another question for every question raised. Your job is to make the students' thinking visible – not your thinking or knowledge at this point!
- Ask each member what he or she thinks. Ask what the group thinks.
- Begin the inquiry with simple processes like describing the scenario in the students' own words and linking it to their own experience and prior knowledge. Note that the initial experience can be frustrating.
- Get some (the better ones), if not all the groups, to share their problem statements.
- Emphasize that this is the beginning of their self-directed learning journey and that they are to deliberate and inquire further. Suggest a fixed amount of self-directed learning time (e.g. two hours) when it comes to allocation of self-directed deliberation and information search pertaining to the problems.

Experiencing PBL

Suppose you are part of a PBL group and you are presented with the following "mosquito problem".

There is an explosion of mosquitoes in a suburban region of Kampala, Uganda. Local news report that several villages and towns there have been under siege from disease-carrying mosquitoes. According to a report from a nearby medical centre, a number of people have been hospitalized. The usual methods of mosquito control do not seem to be effective. You are with a group of humanitarian volunteers and workers. The group has been approached to help with the problem. You have access to further support, resources and funding. What recommendations would you make to help solve the problem?

Read through the problem several times and think through before reading further. What comes to your mind? How would most people approach such a problem?

I have used such problems many times in workshops with students, teachers and educators. In about 80 per cent of the cases, the participants addressing this problem would come up with (1) a list of issues from their brainstorming and discussion and (2) a list of causes and solutions, a typical example of which is shown in Table 4.2.

There is nothing wrong with coming up with a list of issues or one identifying possible causes and solutions. What is often missing, however, is a thorough listing of the facts of the problem before going into identifying the causes. The problem with mere brainstorming of ideas is that it is often not followed by a systematic distinction of facts, hypotheses and ideas.

In PBL, the first stage is to teach the identification of the problem based on *facts*. Instead of stating the facts that we know or seeking additional information or more accurate data, people often move straight into hypothesizing causes and suggesting solutions. There is also a tendency to perceive a problem with a sweeping or biased perception. This first stage also entails getting students to inquire and

Table 4.2 Typical output from group problem solving

Causes	Solutions
Wet season	Massive clean-up
Stagnant water	Regular pest control
No proper fumigation	Enforcement of health laws
Lack of manpower	Education
Poor housing conditions	
Poor habits of people	
Poor drainage system	
Ignorance of conditions for mosquito breeding	
Financial constraints	

to learn to *ask questions* to obtain an accurate and thorough understanding of the problem.

Table 4.3 summarizes the key practices pertaining to the first stage of facilitation of the problem-solving process.

To help students develop a more systematic way of approaching problems, we can encourage the use of templates such as those shown in Figures 4.4(a) to (c). These are just examples of typical templates used in many PBL programmes. Depending on the nature of the problem and the preference of the team, any of these can be used. Other refinements and innovations are also possible (as in Figure 4.4d).

The purpose of these templates is to help us:

- clarify facts (what we know) from ideas
- identify what further data or information we may need
- identify knowledge gaps
- list new learning we need to attain (learning issues)
- clarify things to be done

For the mosquito problem, a KNL chart may look like Table 4.4. Similarly, we can encourage better analysis in the solution phase by using a template that comprises strategies, pros, cons and consequences, such as Table 4.5.

Table 4.3 Facilitating understanding of the problem

This stage involves helping students with the following:
- Reading thoroughly, observing and reflecting (often underlining key facts, making notes and enquiries)
- Learning to clarify and ask questions (e.g. about terms, concepts, assumptions, vagueness and lack of data)
- Overcoming sweeping perceptions and assumptions
- Avoiding unwarranted narrow perceptions and bias
- Developing systematic and thorough information gathering, accuracy, precision, as well as breadth and depth of perception
- Contextualizing and understanding the nature of the problem confronted
- Reframing the problem (it is only when you can state the problem in your own words that you can solve it!)
- Understanding limitations (knowing things beyond our control)
- Understanding delimitations (the need to deliberately define the scope of problem solving or work within the available expertise or resources)
- Using questions to identify (and state) the problem
- Asking why and why-not questions

What we **know**	What we **need** to know	**Learning** issues

(a) A KNL template

List of **ideas**	List of **facts**	**Learning** issues

(b) An IFL template

What is the **situation in need of improvement**?	Hypotheses	Learning needs

(c) A SINI template

We **know**	Our **ideas**	We **need** to know	Our to **do** list

(d) A KIND template

Figure 4.4

Table 4.4 A KNL chart for the mosquito problem

What we know	What we need to know	Learning issues
Explosion in mosquito population	Extent of the population explosion	How mosquitoes multiply in this region
Site of outbreak – Kampala, Uganda	Geography, ecology and environment of the areas affected	Geographical and demographic patterns of city; urban development plans
Several villages and towns affected	Species of mosquitoes and their effects on humans	Information on the species of mosquito causing the outbreak; its reproduction and life cycle; conditions that encourage breeding; impact on the health of people and the diseases caused
A number of people have been hospitalized	Available hospital treatment and medical help for victims	Methods of chemical and biological control to eradicate problem and prevent future outbreaks
Usual methods of mosquito control ineffective	The "usual" control methods (e.g. frequency of spraying) and why they are ineffective	Knowledge of types of insecticides and their effects
Our role – to investigate problem and find solutions	How to control the spread and eliminate the mosquitoes	How to increase public awareness through the use of campaigns, public forums and health screening
Availability of additional support, resources and funding	Current hygiene levels, health habits, practices, existing public campaigns and education	How to remove stagnant water and other breeding grounds and how to improve drainage systems and sanitation
	Current state of living conditions and drainage systems	Relative cost-effectiveness of methods of eradication
	Extent of political drive/involvement to improve conditions	Health management system – political and financial costs
	Preventive treatment and costs. What resources are available: budget, equipment, chemicals, pesticides, manpower, health and medical expertise, etc.	Budget planning

Table 4.5 Solution matrix for mosquito problem

Strategy	Pros	Cons	Consequences
Fumigation	Immediate action Covers a wide area	Inconvenience to residents Stoppage of activities in fumigated areas	Causes respiratory problems Loss of valuable man-hours
Public education	Long-term solution Preventive measure Increases awareness	Lukewarm response May not reach target audience Effect not immediate Time consuming and expensive	Decreases occurrences in the future Ensures continuity of awareness Raises civic consciousness
Punitive measures	Highlights seriousness of problem Minimizes irresponsible actions in the future	Public outcry Political repercussions Opposition from pressure groups	Raises funding for research Ensures better working conditions Raises civic consciousness
Health screening	Prevents further loss of lives Prevents spread of diseases	Expensive Inconvenient Strain on health department resources	Lives saved Saves on medical costs in the long run
Research and development	Long-term solution Creates database Better response in the future Possible cheaper innovations	Expensive Expertise needed Resources needed Not immediate solution	Experience gained May discover new species Increases reputation in the international research community

Table 4.5 (continued)

Strategy	Pros	Cons	Consequences
Neighbourhood "mosquito" wau;h	Promotes neighbourliness Пong-term preventive measure Encourages responsibility within community Promotes civic-mindedness	Not immediate Poor response Neighbours may turn on one another Troublesome for residents	Better or more hostile environment Builds or strains social relationships Decreases costs
Biological control methods such as the use of fish or frogs	Avoids harmful effects of insecticides	Overbreeding of frogs or fish	Ecological imbalance may lead to catastrophe Environment-friendly
Increased frequency of fogging	Kills mosquitoes effectively	Air pollution Health hazards	Health problems
Frequent inspection of possible breeding sites	Early detection Effective control	More manpower needed Increased costs to authority	Manpower stretched leading to stress Coordination problems
Regulatory control of breeding at construction sites	Reduces absenteeism of construction workers due to diseases	Increased costs to construction firms	Greater awareness of the importance of controlling breeding of pests

The above are just examples of how templates can be used to facilitate and scaffold inquiry and learning. Depending on the level of maturity of the students, different templates can be used. Templates can also be used to help students manage their time and learning tasks. For example, a PBL work plan may include these elements:

- List of things to do
- By whom
- By when
- Resources needed

In PBL, the tutor thus manages the learning environment to encourage students' engagement with and immersion in the problem. The tutor also plays an active role in facilitating collaborative inquiry and students' learning process.

5

PROBLEM-BASED LEARNING AND HIGHER-ORDER THINKING

Cognitive-centred Learning Processes

The development of problem-solving acumen and of competencies for creative problem solving is an important goal of PBL. This requires the PBL tutor or coach to intervene in many thinking (cognitive and metacognitive) processes.

The processes that follow engagement of the problem include:

- problem clarification
- problem definition and reframing
- problem analysis
- problem summary and synthesis

In order to clarify, define and reframe the problem in their own words, students should realize the need to take time to think and plan. For example, in the mosquito problem given in the previous chapter, it is not uncommon to find students jumping to conclusions and giving solutions such as how to control dengue fever when they have not even ascertained some of the facts given. The statement that the "usual methods of mosquito control do not seem to be effective" is often overlooked or ignored. Many also do not pay enough attention to other details or raise questions pertaining to the geography and possible implications of the site of occurrence.

Effective problem solving in the real world involves the harnessing of cognitive processes including:

- "planful" thinking (taking time to think and planning)
- generative thinking (coming up with ideas and taking multiple perspectives)

- systematic thinking (being organized, thorough and systematic)
- analytical thinking (classifying, logical analysis and inference)
- analogical thinking (applying similarities, patterns, parallel and lateral thinking)
- systemic thinking (holistic and helicopter thinking)

Cognitive coaching here involves helping students refrain from unplanned (impulsive) reactions, overcoming sweeping perceptions and unwarranted narrow perceptions. By repeatedly querying about the facts to obtain a clear mental picture, problem solvers also learn to develop systematic and more thorough information gathering.

Often PBL problems are designed in such a way that additional data and information are given only when students ask for them. In other words, the "hypertext" has to be identified and asked for. For example, in the mosquito problem, if students ask for details of the geography of Kampala, the information will then be supplied to them.

> **Thinking is infused in PBL when students plan, generate hypotheses, employ multiple perspectives, and work through facts and ideas systematically. Problem resolution also involves logical and critical analysis, use of analogies and divergent thinking, and creative integration and synthesis.**

In nursing education, for instance, we may present a problem based on an emergency scenario.

> *Ah Kow, a polytechnic student, has been rushed to the Accident and Emergency Department at Changi Hospital. He is breathing very rapidly and heavily. He has been camping outdoors at East Coast Beach.*

Further information will be supplied when students ask for it. The purpose is to get students to ask for the patient's medical history. If the additional information given is that "Ah Kow has diabetes", then it becomes much more apparent that the problem could be one of insulin. The students may then suggest an immediate blood test, and the "hypertext" related to this problem scenario would be the laboratory report on the blood test.

PBL processes and coaching involve getting the mind to make connections through reflection, articulation and learning to see different perspectives. In the PBL process, the problem scenario and scaffolding (such as the KIND template and questions posed) help learners develop cognitive connections. Having obtained more data and new information, students need to apply analytical thinking skills, such as comparing, classifying, logical thinking and inferential thinking. Good analytical thinking involves not only logic but also knowing when we have to interpolate and extrapolate.

In his book *Reasoning and Thinking*, Manktelow (1999) noted that a substantial amount of psychological research supports the observation that bias and error in human reasoning are widespread. Jonathan Evans and his colleagues (2002) found in a study of undergraduates that in problem solving there is a tendency for people to focus on a single hypothesis. People also have a tendency to have what he termed "pseudo-diagnostic" response, rather than diagnostic response, based on their background and belief. Evans gave the following example: Suppose a patient has symptom S and the fact is that symptom S is present in 95 per cent of people suffering from disease X. Jumping to the conclusion that the patient is likely to suffer from X without further probing constitutes weak reasoning. Whether the patient is suffering from X would in fact be dependent on at least two further questions: (1) the prevalence of X relative to other diseases and (2) the likelihood of S being present in other diseases.

My point is that there is a need to emphasize the learning of problem solving through facts and rationality. That weak thinking is prevalent is supported by psychological research. The PBL process and coaching help develop flexibility and helicopter views by enhancing connectivity as illustrated in Figure 5.1.

Enhancing connectivity in thinking includes:

- connecting with prior knowledge
- connecting with prior experiences
- connecting with the real-world context
- connecting with theories
- connecting with other people's perceptions
- connecting with new facts and ideas

Recent studies such as that by Chin and Brewer (2001) reveal that data evaluation should be the central goal of student learning. When it comes to solving a problem, the ability to construct an accurate model and to elaborate on the model is often limited. There is also

The ability to make intelligent connections is a key to problem solving in the real world. Cognitive coaching in PBL helps enhance connectivity in data collection and in elaboration and communication of information.

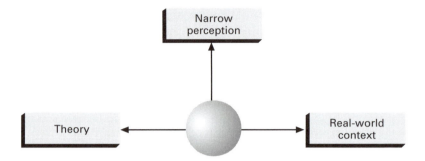

Default connectivity in thinking with tendency towards tunnel perception and weak connection to context

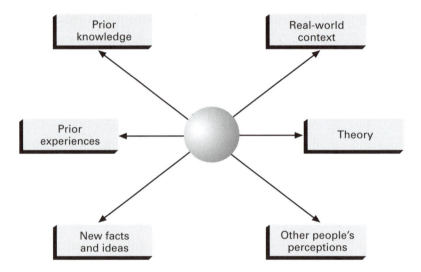

Enhanced connectivity in thinking with multiple and helicopter perceptions and harnessing of resources

Figure 5.1 Connectivity in thinking

evidence that poor problem solving occurs because of the tendency to accept or reject particular key linkages. In other words, a set of cognitive strategies (such as those pertaining to searching for alternative causes and so on) to deal effectively with a given set of data is often lacking. Studies such as that of Lee and Anderson (2001) point to the idea that multiple mechanisms are at work when people work on tasks and fluency in performance can be developed through exercising of general strategies and appropriate attention shifts. PBL trains students to develop and internalize problem-solving competencies by increasing their awareness of different ways of thinking needed in working on a problem.

Effective facilitation of PBL thus involves cognitive coaching and intervention. In my research based on the cognitive theories of Robert Sternberg of Yale University and Reuven Feuerstein of the International Center for the Enhancement of Learning Potential, I have identified many key cognitive functions in problem solving as shown in Figure 5.2.

Previous studies in psychology such as those of Bourne and colleagues (1979), West and Pines (1985), and Sternberg and Davidson (1995) have highlighted the importance of paying attention to cognitive processes to enhance learning and problem solving. In the model of cognitive coaching in PBL shown in Figure 5.2, I have also

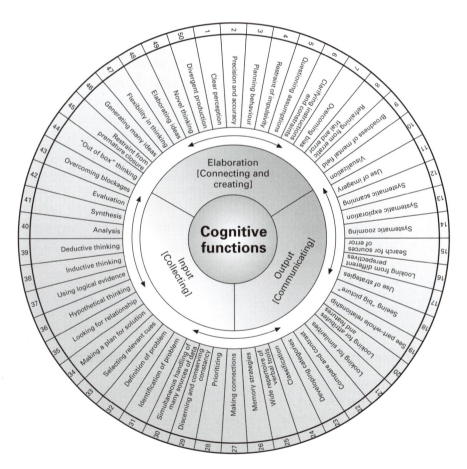

Figure 5.2 Cognitive coaching in problem solving (source: Tan, 2000a)

highlighted the importance of looking at thinking using a refinement of the information processing model that I have called the 3Cs: (1) collecting information, (2) connecting information, and (3) communicating information.

Lapses in reasoning and good thinking can occur in any of these phases of information processing. The practice of scanning the information field, paraphrasing, dialogue, peer critique, and articulation in PBL helps sharpen thinking in collecting, connecting and communicating information.

Facilitation of Thinking

The PBL cycle also includes:

- formulation of learning objectives
- acquisition of new information (following self-directed learning)
- new iteration of problem analysis
- problem solution
- review and evaluation of solution

Table 5.1 summarizes the key processes in the PBL problem resolution process.

The tutor's role is to mediate learning by probing and questioning to facilitate learning of key concepts, principles and theories. The tutor scaffolds, bridges and closes gaps in guiding students towards learning what is important in solving the problem and in acquiring knowledge in the disciplines concerned. In tutorials, a variety of cooperative learning approaches can be used to make collaboration interesting and productive. The tutor encourages comprehensive coverage and critical evaluation of information and research resources.

One of the greatest challenges in working with PBL approaches in the curriculum is facilitating inquiry for deeper learning (Gallagher et al., 1992). I have come across PBL classes that were not effective because the tutors failed to facilitate the necessary inquiry. The

Facilitating inquiry for deeper learning is a major challenge. Effective PBL tutoring employs a good range of scaffolding and questioning techniques. Effective scientists, entrepreneurs and decision makers know how to ask good questions to help arrive at solutions. The goal of inquiry in PBL is to help students internalize such dialogues.

Table 5.1 Facilitation of PBL problem resolution process

Problem analysis
- Cognition: connecting with prior knowledge (3Cs activated), further clarification, scanning–spanning–searching, "organizational" thinking, systematic exploration, open-mindedness, creativity and divergence
- Tutor's prompting to ensure key areas to be learnt are not overlooked

Problem summary and synthesis
- Overview of what has been analysed and hypothesized
- Articulation and summarizing of key information
- Clarity of mental field and mental representation of problem
- Systematic and systems (holistic) thinking

Students' formulation of learning objectives
- Commitment to the cause of the problem
- Ownership of roles and responsibilities
- Zeroing in on what is important to know and learn
- Gaps in knowledge formulated as learning issues (in the form of questions)
- Learning issues aligned and connected to context
- Learning issues can be multidisciplinary

Self-directed learning and self-study
- Activation of prior knowledge and goal-directed reading
- Immersion in the relevant resources (e.g. Internet, reference material)
- Learning with a view to sharing
- Evaluating sources of information

Reporting to the group
- Learning by teaching others
- Articulation and paraphrase of knowledge acquired
- Demonstration of mastery of knowledge

Iteration of group problem solving
- Integration of knowledge from different disciplines
- Correction of misconceptions
- Explanation as well as application of knowledge from various sources to solve the problem
- Critique of value, validity and reliability of information and resources brought to the group
- Application of new knowledge to the problem
- Reflection and critique of prior thinking and knowledge
- Doing all the necessary learning and developing new hypotheses in the light of new learning

Review and evaluation
- Closure: tutor's summarization and integration of what has been learnt (major principles, concepts, gaps, etc.)
- Evaluation of PBL processes (e.g. problem solving, self-directed learning, group support and teamwork)

---

students complained to me and called the tutor "Mr What Do You Think" because the tutor repeatedly asked one and only one question: "What do you think?" Many of us are not used to using an inquiry mode of teaching and facilitation. Much staff development will be needed in this area.

Chi and his colleagues (2001) reported that the interactive style of dialogue can be a very effective form of learning, provided the tutor exercises a good amount of scaffolding through good questions.

Table 5.2 provides examples of questions tutors may use in coaching the various PBL stages. The list is not meant to be exhaustive and merely serves to help tutors devise more of their own questions.

Table 5.2 Examples of questions to facilitate inquiry

Meeting the problem	What are your thoughts on this scenario? What comes to your mind? What do we know? What are the statements of facts we can identify? What is meant by the sentence...? What do you think about that statement? Do you have any idea about this term (concept, etc.)? Could you explain what is meant by the term (concept, etc.)?
Problem summary	How would you paraphrase...? Describe in your own words... Describe the sequence: what came/happened first...followed by what? What can we say about the who, when and where? Could you restate what the group discussed? Does the group have the same mental picture of...?
Problem analysis	What can we make out from the information? What additional information might we need? What do we need to know? Can we know for certain...? Could you think of anything else? What does that link you to? Have you considered all the possibilities? Do we have enough data/knowledge to suggest that...?

Formulation of learning objectives	What is important for you to solve the problem? Have you listed all the key questions? Why do you think this issue is important? What makes you include...? What kinds of resources might be helpful?
Bringing new knowledge and problem solution	Describe what you have learnt about... Explain what you understand by... Specifically, what do you mean by...? How do you know? Could you elaborate on...? How valid and reliable is this? How would you connect what you learnt to...? How does it work? Why is it so? Explain the strategy... Explain your solution... What is at stake if we do this...? What is at stake if we do not...? What are the pros and cons? What are the consequences? What would the end product look like?
Review and evaluation	What are three key things you have learnt about the problem? What did you learn about yourself and your peers? What did you learn about your problem-solving approaches? What did you learn about your independent learning? How different would it be if..? What other sources and counterchecks do you have? What solution might you propose to meet the following criteria? How do you apply it to another situation? What other follow-up might you recommend? If you'd do it again, what might you do more/less? How might you do it differently the next time?

Mediated Learning in PBL

The characteristics of effective PBL coaching can be summarized by the mediated learning experience (MLE) model. First expounded by Professor Reuven Feuerstein (Feuerstein, 1990; Feuerstein & Feuerstein, 1991), the model has been represented by Tan (Tan, 2000a; Tan et al., 2003) as shown in Figure 5.3. It captures the key

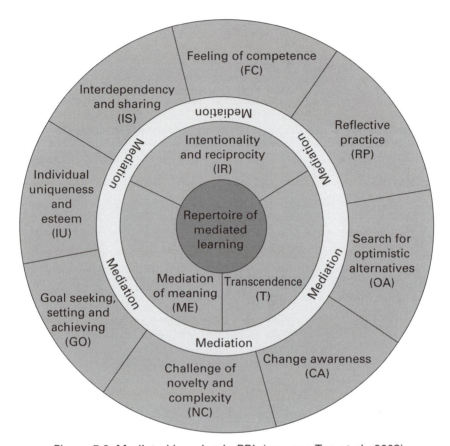

Figure 5.3 Mediated learning in PBL (source: Tan et al., 2003)

parameters for teacher interaction with students that promotes inquiry and metacognition. It also takes into consideration the affective and motivational aspects of learning that underpin good PBL.

As in all good interactive approaches to learning, PBL interactions should include three indispensable characteristics: (1) intentionality and reciprocity (IR), (2) mediation of meaning (ME), and (3) transcendence (T).

In terms of the first characteristic, the PBL tutor should have a clear intention of what inquiries to elicit. Reciprocity refers to the tutor's alertness and awareness of how the learner responds to the intention of the PBL process. The presence of this IR parameter implies that an explicit and purposeful outcome should result from the interaction. PBL tutors need to be clear about their intentions and the outcomes, such as learning of content, problem-solving skills and lifewide skills as described in the earlier chapters.

The next major characteristic is the mediation of meaning. In any learning situation, the awareness of meaning constitutes a major component of the motivation system. The reason problem scenarios are powerful is because of the real-world context and the meaningfulness they present. In the coaching and probing process, many why-questions are raised. An effective mediator helps the learner discover the significance of working on such a problem as well as the value of the PBL process.

Transcendence refers to the transfer of learning across contexts and situations. One main reason PBL is advocated in many curricula is its effectiveness in bringing about transfer of learning. Students learn to take a lifewide approach to learning so that they actually learn how to learn.

These three parameters (IR, ME and T), represented in the inner ring of Figure 5.3, are necessary and sufficient conditions for MLE. The other parameters are often present whenever applicable in effective learning situations. Mediation of feelings of competence (FC) relates to the need to provide "successful experiences" in the tasks given to students and to remove the unwarranted fear of failure. FC is important as the fear of making mistakes often results in a lack of commitment to try again. The purpose of scaffolding is to help develop the sense of competence in problem solving.

In PBL, tutor–learner and learner–learner dialogue and questions are a cornerstone of learning. We ask questions such as: What comes to your mind as you approach the problem scenario? What are your hypotheses? What strategies might we use? What might you do differently if the criteria are now changed? This is the mediation of reflective practice (RP), which relates to self-regulatory and metacognitive behaviours. Metacognition is an essential competence in PBL, as pointed out by Gijselaers (1996).

Mediation of interdependence and sharing (IS) refers to a "sense of belonging" and sharing behaviour. We have already mentioned the importance of collaboration and that one of the roles of the PBL tutor is to broaden students' perspectives on learning. When it comes to understanding a real-world situation and getting a full perspective, "none of us is as smart as all of us". Furthermore, the ability to harness information from others and build a pool of people resources is a life skill. The tutor in PBL encourages students to get out of their comfort zones and learn to seek information from various sources and from people. Teamwork, interdependence and knowledge sharing are attributes emphasized in today's world.

The formulation of learning issues in PBL, the need to teach one another and the challenge of solving a real-world problem provide strong goal-directed behaviours (GO). The tutor's role is to guide and ensure that individuals and groups are constantly engaged in such goal-seeking and goal-attaining behaviours. Good PBL programmes must also offer sufficient challenge and novelty, hence the NC parameter. After all, PBL is about enhancing intelligence to confront ill-structured and novel problems.

The repertoire of MLE in Figure 5.3 is meant to be a simplified map to enable PBL tutors to focus on key behaviours. For example: Is the learning purposeful, meaningful and transferable? Does the learning environment encourage feelings of competence, goal-seeking behaviours and the need for challenge and novelty? Are we optimizing learning by emphasizing heuristics, scaffolding and connecting students to important milieus of knowledge? Do the PBL process and design encourage development of collaborative and peer learning?

To summarize, PBL facilitators need to bear in mind the quality of interaction, inquiry and thinking. We should use the PBL process to make students' thinking "visible" so that we can encourage deeper learning.

> **PBL is about making students' thinking visible and stretching multiple ways of thinking to confront problems that are ill-structured and novel. PBL coaching involves active mediation of purpose, meaning, transfer of learning, optimistic seeking of alternatives, goal-directedness, challenge, collaboration and self-reflection.**

6

DESIGN OF PROBLEMS

Roots of Problem Design

In the late 1980s, whilst working as a mathematics educator, I was dissatisfied with the way mathematics was taught, particularly the overemphasis on drill and practice, learning by memorization and number crunching. What followed was my co-authorship of a series of mathematics textbooks published in the early 1990s entitled *Mathematics: A Problem-solving Approach.* In the preface to teachers in Book 2 of the series, I wrote: "The societal and industrial changes of our time ... call for an educational system that will increasingly produce 'thinkers' and problem solvers" (p. vii). The problem-solving approach I took in the book was inspired by the works of the Budapest-born mathematician George Polya (1887–1985), who advocated a four-step approach to a problem: (1) understand the problem, (2) decide on a plan, (3) carry out the plan, and (4) look back and reflect. What I like about Polya's ideas are the heuristic approach (looking at strategies) and the development of rules of discovery and invention.

Apart from emphasizing the problem-solving process, the other thing I did was to make mathematics applicable to everyday life by using real-world problems. I presented problems involving floor plan calculations, costing, loans and interest computations and so on, where applicable. Similarly, problems of real-world surveys and statistics were incorporated where relevant. Those were puny efforts and the impact was marginal as there were limitations to what one could put in textbooks.

In the mid-1990s, as a staff developer in a newly established higher education institution, I tried to advocate the use of teaching methodologies that would engage active learning and thinking through the use of cases, simulations and problems. Although I was aware of the potential of the use of problems at that time, I did not put much thought into the use of real-world problems in relation to the larger goals of education.

Having worked in tertiary education for some time, my observations concur with those of Robert and Michele Root-Bernstein (1999), who noted that "disconnection between academic knowledge and physical experience continues to plague education today" (p. 17). The Bernsteins cited professors from some of the best universities lamenting about students who had mastered calculus in final examinations but were unable to apply the calculus to the solution of practical problems in physics.

The roots of problem design are real-world problems. It seems obvious and common sense that engineering professors should be teaching students how to deal with the engineering problems that engineers face in industry today. The medical faculty should be teaching students the problems of medicine that they will encounter in practice, including how to deal with new diseases where remedies have yet to be found. The teacher educator should be showing trainee teachers how to handle situations in the real world of the classroom (Robinson, 1993). Yet, all too often the gap between theory and practice remains.

It is interesting to consider the history of higher education. Universities were traditionally hubs of philosophies, deep thinking and inquiry. In the early days, many philosophers in the sciences were also scientists who made great discoveries of natural laws and principles and laid the foundations of the scientific approach and the rigours of inquiry. Developments in the arts, humanities and political and social sciences have similar beginnings in the universities where critical thinking, reasoning and appreciation made their mark. I am presenting an oversimplified picture here. It can be said, however, that traditionally professional education was about apprenticeship. The training of engineers, medical doctors, architects, accountants, legal professionals and so on had its beginnings in the apprenticeship form of learning. The apprentice learnt by seeing how experts solved real-world problems and subsequently taking up the problems themselves. When professional training was incorporated into higher education, the training process was meant to accelerate learning as well as inject multidisciplinary and deeper reasoning and inquiry. Real-world problem solving in the apprenticeship model was not meant to be replaced. One can get caught up here with the debate on the dangers of academics becoming more engaged in problems that could easily yield journal papers than keeping in touch with real-world problems in their professions. The point I would like to make, however, is the need to be cognizant of real-world problems and challenges in order to bring good problems into the curricula.

I mentioned in Chapter 3 that in the early years in Europe technical universities in Denmark and the Netherlands had a tradition of giving students problems that were encountered in industry then. It was of course not uncommon for professors in these institutions to have a foot in both industry and the universities. A few years ago, I had the opportunity to discuss with Professor Dietmar von Hoyningen-Huene, Rector of Fachhochschule Mannheim (a university of applied science in Germany), about the challenges of education for the future. We noted that it is really important for academics to be exposed to the latest problems in their industry and that any chasm between academics and professionals would only render the former obsolete.

The thought about using problems as an innovation in education came to me when I was visiting Chicago in 1999. It probably helped when one was sitting by the Great Lake Michigan and enjoying the summer breeze in that windy city. I had just visited some of the splendid museums and enjoyed the city tour. The city of Chicago, with its many magnificent buildings, is itself a great site and museum of modern architecture. It is well known that about 130 years ago the Great Chicago Fire devastated and destroyed everything in that city. The devastation became an opportunity for the city to rebuild in new ways. Chicago is the birthplace of the skyscraper, and its architects initiated international architectural styles and movements that continue to inspire budding architects. Perhaps we need a fresh approach to education, I thought. Perhaps change should be more drastic than incremental. Perhaps we need to innovate the academic architecture.

Incidentally, it was in Chicago where I first held discussions with Dr Martin Ramirez, President and Chief Learning Officer of IDEAS at Naperville, Illinois. We talked about problem solving in the real world, educational reforms to transform learning and particularly about how to use real-world problems for learning. A who's who in science and engineering, Martin had helped the Illinois Mathematics and Science Academy (IMSA) develop and use PBL for their K–12 curricula. IMSA has since become a centre known for its effective use of PBL in secondary school curricula. In our conversations, we became convinced that the ability of educators to make use of problems creatively would be a major aspect of educational innovation in the 21st century. That year I also met some of the PBL-pioneering staff at IMSA and observed how educators themselves were refreshed and challenged as they sought to bring contemporary and relevant problems into the curriculum. The need for educators to design and bring

> **The roots of problem design are real-world problems. Professors need to have up-to-date knowledge of the problems that professionals in their disciplines are working on today. Teachers need to be in touch with real-world challenges in the society. The ability of educators to use problems creatively is a major aspect of educational innovation.**

good problems to their students means that they have to be constant learners themselves to be in touch with the challenges of society and industry.

What Constitutes a Problem?

According to Michael Hicks (1991), four things are implicit when we talk about a problem: (1) we recognize that there is a problem, (2) we do not know how to resolve the problem, (3) we want to resolve it, and (4) we perceive that we are able to find a solution. A problem presented to students in PBL should therefore evoke a recognition of the problem, an awareness of the existing gap in the students' knowledge, a willingness to resolve the problem and a perception that they can find a solution. In many cases, it also implies that they are able to implement the solution. The following are examples of the types of problem triggers and stimuli.

Failure to Perform

A problem could be a malfunctioning system. It could be something that is not working according to order. It could be a person's performance that falls short of expectation.

For example, in a vehicle servicing course, the trainer can present a real-world problem that trainees will face:

> *Jane has a four-year-old car. She has just attended a meeting in town and discovered that she could not start her car.*

In a computer engineering course, students could be given circuit plans and diagrams of a local area network together with a problem like this:

The company Total Ed Consultants Pte Ltd has a network of computers as shown in the given diagrams. The various systems in the network have been gradually upgraded and have been in operation without major problems in the last two years. Recently, the entire network has drastically slowed down, possibly due to virus attacks.

In a teacher education course on teaching thinking, a problem like the following could be posed:

Ms Sally Lin has taught normal-stream students at both lower and upper secondary levels for the past two years. She finds that these students often have difficulty learning concepts and content in mathematics (the subject she is responsible for). It appears to her that many of the intuitive thinking processes and habits that she takes for granted are often not in the repertoire of the students' thought processes. For example, the students are not systematic and analytical. Furthermore, they do not plan or check and would not persist in working towards solutions. She is wondering what she should do.

Situations in Need of Immediate Attention or Improvement

There are many problems in the world that are situations in need of immediate help and improvement, such as hunger, poverty, lack of health care, and diseases. In PBL, however, the problem situation presented should be specific. Many problems in medicine and nursing are presented as situations in need of immediate attention. For example:

Mr Power Eski, 33, a marketing manager, has just arrived at the airport from Hong Kong. He has difficulty breathing and appears to have a fever.

Generally, a situation in need of improvement draws on disciplinary knowledge to understand the nature and context of the problem and requires systematic problem solving or intervention.

In a course on counselling skills for management, a scenario such as the following may be presented. In this case, the scope of learning issues expected may include understanding personality, working style and workplace counselling techniques.

Ms SS (37 years old) and Ms AK (32 years old) are lecturers in an engineering department of a polytechnic. SS is a coordinator of one of the engineering modules and has been with the polytechnic for four years, while AK has been there for one year. Both have working experience in the private sector but decided to join the polytechnic for a more stable career. The head of department has just discovered that they have not been talking to each other when he assigned SS to form a task force with a number of staff and SS insisted that AK be excluded. The head of department, on further probing and talking to staff, found that AK and SS have been having communication problems since day one.

According to AK, SS has been totally unhelpful from day one and has turned her away many times when she tried to be friendly. She was not even asking for help but needed to find out about the programme from her. She has heard that SS is very ambitious, only "socializes upwards", is cold and does not share with her colleagues.

AK, however, has now found her own circle of friends from the department and feels that she does not need to go to SS anymore.

According to SS, AK expected hand-holding from day one and wanted to be given all the details of what and how to teach. Everything was given to her through e-mail attachments, although all the information she wanted is on the Web and she could have checked it out herself. Other new lecturers do not need to ask the kinds of questions she asked. AK had on several occasions put the blame on the coordinator when she failed to pay attention to notices given. There were several finger-pointing incidents and AK went around talking behind her back about things that were not accurate.

If you were the head of department, how can you help them?

A course in logistic operations may have a problem scenario such as this:

The engineers in a computer manufacturing plant are increasingly frustrated that the gains they have achieved at their plant are being frittered away in the distribution system. Some 30 per cent of the cost of the product has been attributed to distribution and sales.

Finding Better and New Ways to Do Things

Often, normal-functioning business operations and operation systems present a problem situation where we want to raise standards, improve quality or obtain better results. Many businesses have to continually improve their company image, create higher value and so on in order to survive. Similarly, companies often seek to improve their operation systems in terms of reducing cycle time, eliminating errors and so forth. Rather than teaching the subject matter and content, we could present relevant cases, data and information to students. The students' knowledge gaps will create the need for learning the content and at the same time stretch their creativity in applying the knowledge.

For example, detailed reports of an anonymous company can be given, such as its annual report, balance sheet and profiles of its management team. The problem could be posed as follows:

XYZ is a private limited company whose major products and services are as given in the portfolio and reports. It plans for public listing to raise funds of $50 million for international expansion. You and your team members are tasked by the management consultancy you work for to undertake feasibility studies and present reports and executive summaries based on the studies.

In an electrical engineering course, students can be provided with detailed building and electrical plans of the air-conditioning circuitry, power consumption reports together with a problem as follows:

ABC is a plant that manufactures special computer chips. In the current system, most of the air-conditioning in the plant is left on 24 hours. You have been tasked to propose improvement to the existing systems and to install new controls to reduce electricity consumption in the long run.

Unexplained Phenomena or Observations

It has been said that discovery is seeing what everybody has seen and thinking what nobody has thought of. Breakthroughs in science and technology are often a result of understanding phenomena and observations. Problems can be presented in the form of a phenomenon or observations and students are required to seek explanations to these observations. In some cases, it could be problems where causes are actually unknown and current explanations lacking.

Science is full of such inquiries as: How does a dragonfly remain stationary in the air? The problem presentation could be accompanied by field trips to watch dragonflies in action. Depending on the age group of the students, the level of the problem and the innovativeness of the teacher, a simple problem like this can stimulate a great deal of learning. Students could take photographs and videos of dragonflies to study their motion. This may sound like a trivial expansion of a natural phenomenon, but scientists have just recently applied successfully the secret of the dragonfly to fighter jet flying. You see, dragonflies are able to dart to and fro at high speeds to target their prey despite having very delicate bodies. Their secret lies in a water sac. Fighter jet pilots executing diving manoeuvres while flying at high speeds experience a tremendous gravitational force, which pulls the pilot's blood downwards from the head to the toes. This often triggers life-threatening tunnel vision and blackout. This force is many times what you would experience on the most challenging drop on a roller coaster. By copying the dragonfly's way of battling gravity, flying suits were designed with liquid-filled channels. The liquid in the suit's web of channels rushes to the pilot's feet as the gravitational force increases, squeezing their legs tightly so that blood stays at the top of the body. This high-speed flying suit thus protects pilots in their daredevil zooming.

Many problems in science can be presented, such as:

- Why do air bubbles in a tank appear to grow bigger as they rise from the bottom towards the surface?
- Can we produce a magnetic field without using any iron?
- If we use a magnifying glass under water, how will its magnifying power be affected?
- How does a hurricane come about? Can we know when one is coming?

A trigger in a biology or physiology course could be as follows:

It has been claimed that nitric oxide is of great biological importance. You are working as a research assistant, and you have been asked to provide as much accurate information as possible from reported research on how nitric oxide might be produced in the human body and how it affects the various systems and functions of the body.

Apart from scientific and natural phenomena, similar problems could be used for social sciences. For example, a problem such as this may be posed in a psychology course:

We all know that children play. Is playing important for adults too? H.G. Wells played with models and miniatures all his life – they seemed to be significant inspiration for his war-game stories. The physicist Richard Feynman was once quoted as testifying: "Physics disgusts me a little bit now, but I used to enjoy doing physics. Why did I enjoy it? I used to play with it. I used to do whatever I felt like doing – it didn't have to do with whether it was important for the development of nuclear physics, but whether it was interesting and amusing for me to play with. So I got this attitude – I'm going to play with physics whenever I want to, without worrying about any importance whatsoever."

Incidentally, Alexander Fleming used to play with bacterial paintings produced by brushing variously pigmented bacteria onto agar plates. The bacteria developed colour as they grew, producing a piece of art. His playing got him into trouble with the scientific community of his time. However, it led to the accidental discovery of penicillium and the life-saving penicillin.

Gaps in Information and Knowledge

We can also present the current state of knowledge or the state of the art in practice as a problem in terms of a gap in understanding.

In medical or biological science, we may want to trigger learning about vaccines:

> *Prior to the discovery of the smallpox vaccine by Jenner in 1796, every year about 80,000 people reportedly died from smallpox. Today, smallpox has been practically eradicated. In 1963 the vaccine for measles was developed. However, in the 1990s there continued to be some outbreaks of measles. In 2003 an unusual flu-like disease called severe acute respiratory syndrome (SARS) broke out in Guangdong, China. In less than six months, the virus infected about 7,000 people and caused over 600 deaths across some 30 countries. This new form of atypical pneumonia has a fatality rate estimated at about 15 per cent, and there is widespread concern over the success of containing the virus in the countries affected. Can a vaccine be developed quickly? What do we know about how vaccines were developed in the past? How are new vaccines developed and how do we know if they work?*

The lack of valid and reliable data and information can also be a problem situation. To teach nutrition in secondary schools, we may use a PBL approach by presenting a problem such as the following:

> *Eden Chang is a school badminton player. He is 14 and his coach has mentioned to him about his potential to be selected for the national team. Apart from rigorous training, Eden is wondering if nutrition would help increase his chances. One day he walked into a nutrition store in a shopping centre. The salesperson told him that what he needed was more muscle without gaining a lot of weight. He*

ended up buying a jar of creatine tablets that cost $60 and various other supplements costing $80. Eden learnt subsequently that creatine comprises amino acids and is taken by many athletes. Someone, however, told him that there are side effects and that got him worried. Many athletes are in situations like Eden's. You and your group have been selected as "young scientists" for a project on sports nutrition. Your team has been tasked to come up with a report and presentation to advise school sportsmen and sportswomen on nutrition.

Sometimes habits, routines and practices are taken for granted. However, a junior high school student was concerned and asked: "Does microwave cooking with plastic-wrapped food pose any problem to health?" Such questions can be interesting problems.

Decision-making Problems

In the real world, decision making represents one of the most important forms of challenges. It often involves taking into account rational as well as emotive aspects of reasoning. Issues of policies, public opinions, human rights and ethics are examples that can be used in PBL curricula. Specific issues such as the rights of the minority, the rights of people with disabilities, abortion and euthanasia are often raised in the news. A newspaper cutting on a specific case or incident can be a problem trigger.

Take for example the issue of euthanasia. We can take a newspaper article or use a simulated case scenario such as this:

Ozama's uncle was involved in a truck accident three years ago. He became paralysed from the neck down and recently lapsed into a coma. He is basically kept alive by medical equipment. The medical cost of thousands of dollars each week is putting a heavy strain on the family. Some relatives tell them that it is money thrown down the drain and doctors do not expect him to wake up. The family feels guilty about pulling the plug.

Students in this PBL exercise may want to conduct a survey for the medical authority by inviting people from all walks of life to give their views on euthanasia. They may need to find out what the population thinks and gather facts and information on ethical and moral issues and finally present a case of their own based on their reasons and consensus.

Need for New Design or Invention

Creative problems that lead to a new system design or an invention represent an important category of problems in the knowledge-based economy. Are there new ways of doing things? What are the possible consequences and impacts? Industries and businesses are always looking for new designs, inventions, new combinations, new products, new ways of branding and so on.

In biotechnology, one may pose problem triggers such as the following:

A venture capitalist wants to invest in research on ornamental plants. He is particularly interested in cross-breeding that would produce new flowering plants of multiple forms and colours with characteristics of high rates of flower production, stem resilience, etc.

You are with a team of researchers investigating the composition of the ultimate made-to-order multi-vitamin, multi-mineral pill, which is customized according to individual DNA profiles.

There is nothing special about a pair of running shoes or a loaf of bread. Yet, we know that new brands, new designs and new features of running and sports shoes appear on the market year after year. Problems could be posed on the incorporation of new features: What else can we put into a loaf of bread apart from vitamins, fruits and nuts? It is amazing when we consider the amount of innovation possible in the food industry.

In a computer programming course, a design problem may be given as follows:

You have been asked to design a Web page for a travel company that will allow clients to book hotels, plane tickets, tours and so on.

In a fashion design course, the design problem may have a scenario like this:

An association for children with disabilities has approached you about designing clothes that would be particularly user-friendly for their children with different physical disabilities.

Depending on the discipline and the relevance, a host of challenges pertaining to new designs or inventions are possible:

A handphone manufacturer is interested in the kinds of additional new features that could be put into a handphone.

To move into an inventive culture, education and training should look at all kinds of problems and learn from problem solving, whether they be situations in need of improvement, better ways of doing things, closing information gaps, understanding a new phenomenon, or new designs or inventions. Such learning should span disciplines, businesses and industries.

Establishing Your PBL Goals

PBL is about using problems to drive and motivate learning. A successful PBL programme entails sufficient planning in the selection, design and development of problems. Whether this is the first time you are introducing PBL into your curriculum or thinking about the kinds of problems to use, the first thing to do is to reflect on your purpose and goals of using PBL. There are many innovative ways to use problems as triggers as noted earlier, as well as a wide variety of learning approaches and outcomes that can be associated with a given problem scenario and trigger.

Your goals for using PBL might include content learning in a specific discipline, multidisciplinary learning, and acquisition of problem-solving skills and lifewide learning skills, as illustrated in Figure 6.1.

Learning of content knowledge is of primary importance in many curricula. Suppose the topic of learning is aerobic and anaerobic systems. We may also want students to learn basic problem

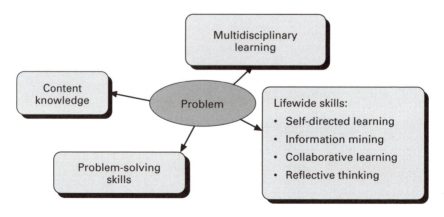

Figure 6.1 Goals of a PBL problem

identification and problem analysis. In PBL, the idea is to look for an unstructured real-world problem to trigger learning. Figure 6.2 represents the PBL goals in this case.

The following is an example of a problem used by the Faculty of Medicine of Maastricht University to address these objectives:

An eight-year-old boy has been submerged in water for more than 15 minutes. Fortunately, a passerby succeeds in getting him out of the water. Mouth-to-mouth resuscitation is applied immediately. Everyone is astonished to see that the boy is still alive.

The problem is unstructured but yields curiosity and inquiry. The cognitive engagements lead to learning issues as students inquire with questions such as:

• How is it possible that the boy is still alive?
• How is it possible for him to recover completely?
• Will there be water in his lungs?

Following such brainstorming and inquiry, students are expected to draw up their learning issues and seek the necessary information on their own. In this case, their learning issues may include the following:

• What is the body's protective mechanism against cold and hypoxia (lack of oxygen)?
• What is the anaerobic system (when the body is not relying on immediate oxygen supply)?
• What happens in the shift from aerobic to anaerobic state?
• Is oxygen needed for energy?

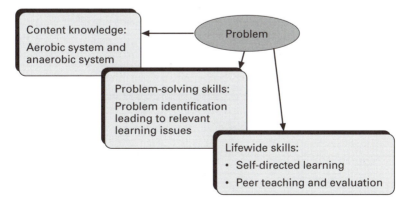

Figure 6.2 Example of the goals of a medical problem

These learning issues should coincide with the content goals and learning objectives of the PBL problem.

Consider the example of the economics problem given in Chapter 3 involving registering and setting up a business. Figure 6.3 illustrates the possible goals of the problem. Apart from acquiring content knowledge, including understanding the purposes and characteristics of sole proprietorships, partnerships, private limited companies and public listed companies, we also want students to take a multidisciplinary perspective where they would learn about setting up a business and apply their writing and communication skills in putting together a business plan and proposal.

Design Features of Problem

Having established the goals of using PBL in your curriculum, the next step is to understand the characteristics of PBL participants, including their profile, prior knowledge, prior experience and their foundation knowledge.

Participants in professional education, for example, often bring with them rich prior experience and knowledge, which can contribute much to the learning process (Tan, 2002b). The nature and complexity of the problem posed will depend very much on the background and profile of the learners. As mentioned earlier, we need to prepare the mindset of students, who are only used to a more didactic mode of

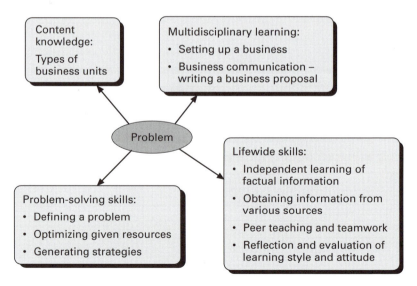

Figure 6.3 Example of the goals of a business problem

learning. We also have to ascertain that students have the basic and foundational knowledge needed to inquire and to understand the problem. It may be necessary to ensure that they are equipped with the basic vocabulary, axioms, principles and tools of a discipline before plunging them into the problem. Productive inquiry cannot take place in a vacuum, and it is important to consider the appropriate level and type of problem to be used to make the most of the PBL experience.

When selecting or designing a problem, several features of the problem have to be considered. These pertain to the problem characteristics, problem context, learning environment and resources, and problem presentation. Table 6.1 summarizes the issues to be considered relating to the characteristics and nature of the problems to be designed.

Once we have a clear goal of using PBL, we think in terms of various problem triggers as illustrated earlier. Real-world problems can be obtained from industry, research literature, news and reports. Students, however, also need to see the real-world relevance of their training programme (Stepien & Gallagher, 1993). PBL instructors should always be on the lookout for potentially good problems and build a portfolio of relevant problems that they can use from time to time.

The problem selected will of course need to be relevant to the curriculum; this will be discussed in the next chapter. The learning issues should be aligned with the learning objectives of the course. One good way to develop the problem is to visualize what students would be going through when they work on the problem. The problem will also need to be delimited in terms of its scope. Will the problem situation be too difficult for students to understand? What about the level of complexity? Does it involve simultaneous handling of too many issues? Do I need to simplify the problem scenario to make it more manageable for students? To what extent is the problem intended to be interdisciplinary? Do I want students to demonstrate their ability to integrate multiple disciplines in solving the problem? Is this a problem with multiple solutions? Do I expect students to decide on one final solution and defend their choice? Is the nature of the problem such that there is only one solution, given the context and constraints? The PBL exercise may also involve empirical collection of data to verify claims, the construction of models or the prototyping of a design or product.

The context of the problem could be highly ill-structured such that it is not immediately obvious what disciplinary knowledge or information bases might be involved. The following are examples of ill-structured problems from the discussion earlier:

Mr Power Eski, 33, a marketing manager, has just arrived at the airport from Hong Kong. He has difficulty breathing and appears to have a fever.

Ms SS (37 years old) and Ms AK (32 years old) are lecturers in an engineering department of a polytechnic . . . The head of department has just discovered that they have not been talking to each other . . .

You are with a team of researchers investigating the composition of the ultimate made-to-order multi-vitamin, multi-mineral pill, which is customized according to individual DNA profiles.

Some problems are less ill-structured in that they are less multi-disciplinary and more focused on a specific discipline. Nevertheless, they could still be good problems. An example is a problem that we encountered earlier:

It has been claimed that nitric oxide is of great biological importance . . . you have been asked to provide as much accurate information as possible from reported research on how nitric oxide might be produced in the human body and how it affects the various systems and functions of the body.

The context presented should create a sense of curiosity and mystery as far as possible. Try to choose contexts that would appeal to students. If possible, state in the problem the roles that students are supposed to play. Ownership, challenge and novelty are essential to motivate maximum engagement by students.

In designing and developing problems, we also need to take into consideration how the problem will engage group and individual learning. Does the problem generate a range of learning issues that require collaboration? Do students need to make use of a substantial amount of primary or secondary sources of information? Is it pragmatic to expect students to get the information on their own? Are the sources of information accessible? Do we need to provide possible sources, such as recommended Web-site links and professionals and experts that they can interview? We also need to consider the time required to address the problem given.

There are many innovative ways to present problems. Although most problems are presented in written form, a variety of presentations are possible. These include problem scenarios, case write-ups, video or audio clips, newspaper cuttings, magazine or journal reports, and news and information from the Web.

Table 6.1 Features of problem design

Problem feature	Issues to address
Characteristics	• What is the real-world relevance of the problem? • What is the curriculum relevance? • What is the level of difficulty? • What is the level of complexity? • Is it an interdisciplinary problem? • Does the problem call for integration of multiple disciplines (or topics)? • How open is the problem (in terms of possible solutions)? • Does it call for a final product?
Context	• Is the problem unstructured (ill-structured)? • Does it trigger curiosity? • Will it motivate ownership? • Does it appear challenging? • Are there sufficient elements of novelty?
Learning environment and resources	• How can the problem stimulate collaborative inquiry? • What kinds of independent learning can be incorporated? • What is the extent of guidance needed for using the learning resources? • What kinds of information resources are expected (e.g. library resources, the Internet)? • Does the problem require further data collection? • Will field work be incorporated? • Will information gathering include interviews and experts' views? • What else might we need to solve the problem?
Presentation	• Do we use a problem scenario? • Should it be a short scene or multiple scenes? • Does the problem scenario come with hypertext? • Do we need a detailed case write-up? • Can we use video clips? • Can we use audio news? • Can we do a role play? • Can we simulate a client requirement? • Are there relevant newspaper cuttings? • What about magazine or journal reports? • Are there Web sites that can be used?

News, current affairs and issues reported on the Web, television, radio or the press are useful sources of problems. Scientific articles as well as industrial and business reports are also rich sources.

Suppose in a nursing course we want to cover the content knowledge of the topic homeostasis with reference to the endocrine, nervous, respiratory and renal systems. At the same time, we want to emphasize problem solving in emergency situations. An example could be the problem given in Chapter 5, which is illustrated in Figure 6.4.

We mentioned that further information would be supplied to students when they ask for it in order to train them in problem

Good problem design takes into consideration:

- **the goals of PBL**
- **students' profiles**
- **problem characteristics: authenticity, curriculum relevance, multiplicity and integration of disciplines**
- **the problem context: ill-structuredness, motivation of ownership, challenge and novelty**
- **the learning environment and resources**
- **problem presentation**

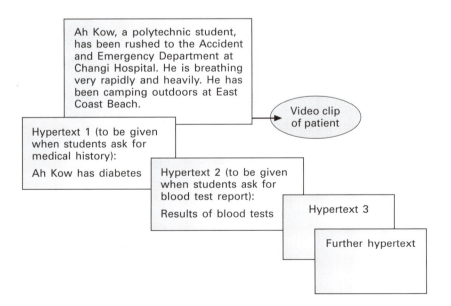

Figure 6.4 Problem presentation in a nursing case

identification. The purpose of this case is to get students to ask for the patient's medical history. The "hypertext" represents further information provided as students ask and inquire.

Finally, when you have designed the problem, it is also good to give an interesting caption or title to the problem. In the next chapter, we will discuss the use of problems designed for larger curricula.

7

CURRICULUM DEVELOPMENT IN PROBLEM-BASED LEARNING

Curriculum Development and PBL

There is a plethora of literature on curriculum development in general and a myriad of curriculum development models of varying complexities. Curriculum development models can take a deductive approach or an inductive approach (Tan, 1994). Deductive models proceed from a general consideration of the needs of society, the professional knowledge required and so on, and move on to the specifics, such as specifying observable learning outcomes. Inductive models start with the actual development of curriculum material and proceed to more global aspects of the curriculum. Whichever approach one takes, there should be three levels of considerations: the mega level (the "why"), the macro level (the "what") and the micro level (the "how"). The "why" takes into consideration the desired graduate profile, the "what" looks at the intended learning outcomes and the "how" concerns designing for the learning. When considering the curriculum, issues that need to be addressed include the following:

- What is the desired graduate profile?
- What are the aims of the programme?
- What are the competencies, knowledge, skills and attitudes to be developed?
- What are the specific goals in the disciplines of the programme?
- For a specific module, what are the syllabus, learning goals, topics and concepts that are important?
- What is the assessment structure?
- How do we monitor and assess students' learning?
- How do we evaluate the effectiveness of the course?

- What are the course structure and the time frame?
- How do we optimize the learning approaches, resources and environment for the desired learning?
- How do we develop the learning packages?
- How do we use PBL to revamp the curricula or infuse it into relevant modules?

Figure 7.1 illustrates these considerations.

Glasgow (1997) observed that most curricula tend to "focus on content coverage and exposing students to wide knowledge base . . . the better models engaged students in problem scenarios that are similar to authentic real-world situations" (p. 13). He advised:

Curricular planners and designers do not have to look any further than the real world, outside institutionalized education frameworks, to find curricular and pedagogical models for relevant learning applications. The bottom line here is that the world is an integrated, multidisciplinary, and interdisciplinary place. It is also filled with problems, projects, and challenges. Beginning to create curriculum that reflects this reality makes sense (p. 14).

In designing problems, we have noted the need to establish our goals for using PBL. Once you have decided on your goals, you need to consider at which level you can introduce PBL into the curriculum. This is illustrated in Figure 7.2. If you are in a position to influence major changes in your institution, you may advocate a change from the mega level, which entails a total revamp of curricula in terms of course structures, assessment structures and the design of the entire learning environment. It is, however, not always easy or necessary to implement PBL at this level, although there are newly established institutions that

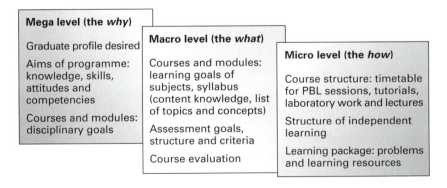

Figure 7.1 Curriculum considerations

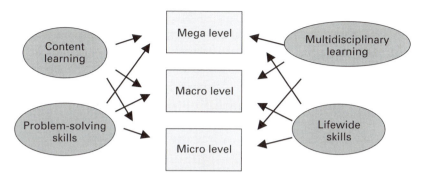

Figure 7.2 Infusing PBL approaches into the curriculum

may be prepared to adopt such challenges, having been convinced of the potential benefits of using PBL approaches. Such implementation would require a great deal of planning, expertise and resources for it to be successful. One should be aware, however, that PBL is not a "one size fits all" methodology. It is more of a philosophy and approach that emphasizes the effective use of problems through an integrated approach of active and multidisciplinary learning. A review of the desired graduate profile of the programme, the nature of the disciplines, disciplinary goals, assessment criteria, current resources and the profile of students is essential to bring about effective introduction of a PBL curriculum. With good planning, management support, resource allocation and staff development, PBL can become a predominant mode of learning supplemented by a range of good instructional methodologies. We have mentioned earlier that many medical schools have successfully adopted PBL in their curricula.

Although the benefits of PBL may be apparent, the practical conversion from a traditional curriculum to a PBL curriculum can be a daunting task owing to administrative and logistic considerations as well as the lack of resources. Therefore, introducing changes at the macro level is more common, where certain courses or modules adopt a PBL approach. Such hybrid approaches may in fact be a promising way to go, as observed by Marincovich (2000). Many high school and secondary school curricula are also restrained by limitations posed by national or state assessment systems and the academic requirements of college entry systems. The lack of curriculum flexibility will limit the ways in which PBL can be used. Nevertheless, there are hopeful signs of gradual change with the diversification of national assessment modes, and PBL will have an increasing role in more innovative education systems.

Teachers can begin at the micro level by using PBL in project work or in certain subjects. However, we do not want too much of the same thing, such as repeating the same emphasis of the PBL cycle in all courses. It may suffice to have a few courses or modules where generic problem solving, collaborative learning and communication are emphasized through the use of PBL approaches. It would be overly repetitive if in every course students have to spend a large amount of time doing peer and group presentations. The key is to use PBL strategically and align the approach with desired educational outcomes.

PBL Curriculum Planning

The first step in planning your PBL curriculum is to align your goals of using PBL with the curriculum goals of your programme. As discussed earlier, this could take place at the mega, macro or micro level. For example, if it is decided that the entire second-year Bachelor of Commerce programme will adopt a PBL approach, we are dealing with changes at a mega level. Suppose only the engineering design and technical communications modules in a third-year engineering course would adopt a PBL approach, the change would be at the macro level with each module lasting 15 weeks or so. PBL is often simultaneously used in general subjects such as service skills, project work or stand-alone electives on creative problem solving. Lastly, PBL can be incorporated at various micro levels as part of a module or for a selection of topics in a subject.

Figure 7.3 depicts the PBL planning and curriculum development process. Like in any standard curriculum development, we start with a statement of the course objectives. Next, we prepare a document that articulates:

- the rationale for using PBL
- what PBL is and what it entails
- PBL goals and outcomes

With a clear idea of where PBL will be incorporated and the likely scope of PBL, we then develop more specific PBL objectives (problem solving, teamwork, presentation skills, etc.) and specific content learning objectives. The scope of learning should then be practically conceptualized in terms of the PBL course structure and time frame. The course structure is usually described in terms of the PBL cycle, such as:

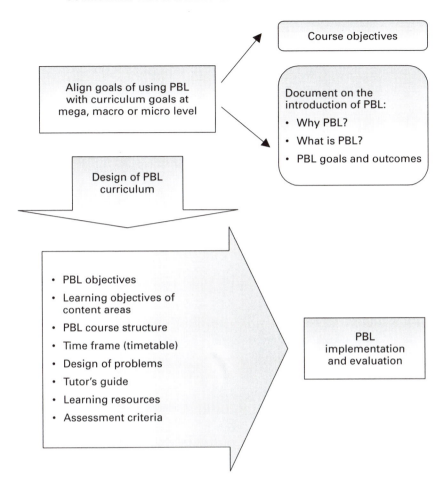

Figure 7.3 Planning a PBL curriculum

- Meet the problem → Problem analysis → Discovery and reporting → Solution presentation → Integration and evaluation
- Meet the problem → Problem inquiry → Generation of learning issues → Discovery and peer teaching → Solution presentation → Review
- Problem encounter → Analysis → Research and field work → Reporting and peer teaching → Presentation of findings → Reflection and evaluation

Many other variations and innovations are possible. The relative emphasis of the PBL stages depends on the PBL goals and the nature of the problem.

To draw up the PBL course structure, we need to decide on the following:

- The nature of the PBL cycle (a schema should be drawn)
- The time frame for the whole cycle and the timetable for each stage
- The PBL tutorial hours, taking into account the time needed for self-directed learning
- The type, scope and number of problems that students will work on

A key step of the PBL curriculum development process is the design of problems, which is usually accompanied by the development of a learning package comprising guides for students and teachers. Included in the guides are key aspects of the learning environment, learning resources and assessment criteria.

It is important to note that assessment often drives learning. Thus, PBL assessment goals should be aligned with the desired outcomes of the curriculum. This means that, besides assessing the acquisition of content knowledge, problem-solving, teamwork and communication skills would also be evaluated. A wide range of assessment methods and strategies will need to be used in PBL, which may include observation charts, reflective journals, checklist on presentation skills, checklist of problem-solving processes, peer assessment and self-assessment.

Finally, it is necessary to evaluate the effectiveness of PBL implementation through a variety of monitoring and evaluation methods. It is only through the implementation of the PBL curriculum and feedback from teachers and students that various aspects of the PBL programme can be fine-tuned and improved.

PBL curriculum development involves a review of the desired graduate profile, examination of the goals and nature of the disciplines, the employment of PBL cycles, and detailing of resources and assessment criteria. Problems are designed such that learning and assessment are aligned with the curriculum goals and PBL goals.

The best way to illustrate how PBL is infused into the curriculum is to look at practical examples of PBL applied in various courses at the macro and micro levels.

Examples of PBL Curricula

Educational Psychology Course

In an educational psychology course for postgraduate trainee teachers, PBL forms 60 per cent of the programme. That means 60 per cent of the course is assessed in terms of PBL. All essential course information, course structure and course assessment are posted on the course Web site, including PBL problems. Students are expected to log on to the Web site to read through the course information and come prepared. Table 7.1 shows a sample of the course objectives.

Table 7.1 Educational psychology course objectives (truncated)

Overall course objectives: Upon completion of the module, student teachers will be able to do the following:
- Appreciate the basic needs and individual differences of students
- Apply theories and principles learnt to their classroom teaching
- Handle students with special needs with sensitivity and understanding

Course objectives: Upon completion of the module, student teachers will be able to do the following:

Attitude
- Appreciate and accept individual differences in students
- Model a positive attitude towards learning and teaching

Skills
- Synthesize the theories learnt and apply them to their classroom teaching
- Model thinking behaviours in classroom teaching
- Reflect on and evaluate their own attitude and performance as trainee teachers

Knowledge
- Explain the developmental needs and individual differences in students
- Analyse cognitive, psychosocial and cultural factors that may facilitate or impede students' development and learning
- Interpret the implications of individual differences in learning and teaching

---

The specific objectives of the PBL components in the course are:

- To articulate the theories of cognitive development. Trainee teachers are expected to be able to describe, explain and apply

the theories of Piaget, Vygotsky and other relevant con-
structivists' theories.

- To articulate learning theories from the perspectives of
  behavioural and cognitive theories. In particular, trainees are
  expected to apply the concepts of (1) classical and operant
  conditioning, social learning and cognitive behaviour
  modification; and (2) information processing, structuring and
  organization of learning and discovery learning.
- To apply reflective, collaborative and self-directed learning
  processes in PBL.

At the start, trainee teachers are given the rationale for a PBL
approach and are told that the programme on learning theories will
not begin with the usual dissemination of content knowledge or
theories. PBL requires a mindset change on the part of students and
calls for initiative, ownership and independence, that is, entrepreneurship. Table 7.2 shows sections on the Web site that give the why
and what of PBL.

Figure 7.4 shows the PBL cycle of the course. Table 7.3 gives the
course structure with the time frame and Table 7.4 shows the guide to
essential reading and suggested resources. Samples of the tutor's guide
are presented in Tables 7.5 to 7.8. In this case, students are required
to work concurrently on three problem scenarios, but the PBL tutor
would subsequently allow students in various groups to focus on
different problem scenarios owing to time constraint. However, by
using a variety of cooperative learning techniques, it is possible to
ensure that students learn from each other how to solve all three
scenarios. The problems designed for this course are real-life classroom
case scenarios. Two of the case scenarios are shown in Figures 7.5 and
7.6. Figure 7.7 provides a sample of the student's guide. The
assessment requirements and criteria are shown in Tables 7.9 and 7.10.

Table 7.2 The why and what of PBL

Why PBL?	What is PBL?

Why PBL?

The course will begin with a problem-based learning (PBL) approach in week 5. Why do we need this curriculum innovation? The Committee on Singapore Competitiveness (Ministry of Trade and Industry, 1998) noted that to "improve the longer-term competitiveness of Singapore, we should refine our education system to help foster creative thinking and entrepreneurial spirit among the young". It stated that three major components of the education system should be addressed, namely, the content of the educational curriculum, the mode of delivering this curriculum to students and the assessment of performance. The Ministry of Education (1998) in a booklet entitled *The Desired Outcomes of Education* listed the goals of post-secondary and tertiary education as, amongst other things, being innovative and having a spirit of continual improvement, lifelong habit of learning and enterprising spirit in undertakings. The challenge is indeed for educators to design new learning environments and curricula that really encourage motivation and independence to equip students with learning and problem-solving skills and competencies that employers are looking for. In a university survey of employers' rating of important skills, the top eight skills in order of importance are teamwork, problem solving, ability to take initiative, desire to learn, interpersonal skills, ability to work independently, oral communication and flexibility in applying knowledge (National University of Singapore, 2000).

The Enterprise Challenge Unit recognized PBL as a useful attempt of educational innovation for the knowledge economy when it gave one of its awards to a PBL innovation in its year 2000 awards. In recent years, there have been a proliferation in the use of PBL amongst professional programmes in areas such as medicine, engineering and business.

What is PBL?

PBL is an educational methodology that emphasizes real-world challenges, higher-order thinking skills, interdisciplinary learning, independent learning, information-mining skills, teamwork and communication skills. In PBL, students experience a problem as the trigger, stimulator and motivator for learning. Students work in small groups to generate hypotheses, identify learning objectives, seek sources of knowledge, evaluate information obtained, reflect, integrate and synthesize plausible solutions. The difference between the traditional approach and the PBL approach can be represented by the three loci of preoccupation as shown.

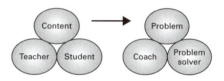

One can no longer expect to have spoon-feeding of notes, summaries and pointers. PBL requires a mindset change on the part of students. It calls for initiative, ownership and independence. This is what entrepreneurship is about. Instead of beginning with content knowledge, you will be confronted with a real-world problem. The problem will be your preoccupation for several weeks of the course. The problem will be an anchor around which you could achieve the learning outcomes of the unit. By working on unstructured problems, you would learn more about learning how to learn. By having real-life problems (rather than content) as focal points, students will take the role of active problem solvers and teachers will act as coaches.

What then would the tutor be doing? Whilst PBL is totally student-centred, the PBL tutor plays the critical role of developing the environment of learning and helps facilitate communication, problem inquiry, critical evaluation and metacognition. In most instances, to every question you ask, the tutor will throw you another question. It may appear difficult and even frustrating at the beginning, but you will really learn and think critically and creatively.

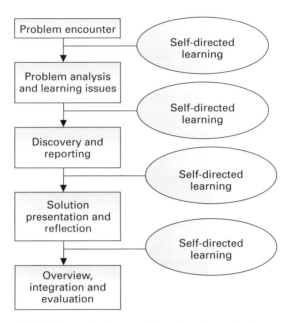

Figure 7.4 PBL cycle for an educational psychology course

Table 7.3 Course outline of the PBL component of an educational psychology course

Week	Course content
Induction week	Introductory lecture PBL preparation
Week 1	Problem encounter • Problem statement • Problem scenario and analysis
Week 2	Problem analysis and learning issues • Identification of learning issues and formulation of learning objectives • Preparation of self-directed learning and peer teaching
Week 3	Discovery and reporting • Report on self-directed learning • Peer teaching
Week 4	Preparation of solution presentation • Group preparation
Week 5	Solution presentation and reflection • Group presentation of findings
Week 6	Overview of learning theories • Q and A • Evaluation

Table 7.4 Guide to essential reading and suggested resources in educational psychology (truncated)

Week	Topic	Essential reading
Week 1	Introduction	Introduction Chapter 1: The teacher as practitioner and researcher See also Web-site guides
Weeks 2–5	Problem scenario 1	Chapter 2: Development theory: cognitive development
	Problem scenario 2	Chapter 6: Learning theories: behaviourism Chapter 7: Cognitive learning theories
	Problem scenario 3	Chapter 4: Exceptionalities: addressing students' unique needs Chapter 5: Student diversity

Suggested references

Tan, O.S., Parsons, R.D., Hinson, S.L., & Sardo-Brown, D. (2003). *Educational psychology. A practitioner–researcher approach (An Asian edition)*. Singapore: Thomson Learning.

Chang, A., Gopinathan, S., & Ho, W.K. (Eds) (1999). *Growing up in Singapore: Research perspectives on adolescents*. Singapore: Prentice Hall.

Chang, A., & Goh, C. (2002). *Teachers' handbook on teaching generic thinking skills*. Singapore: Prentice Hall.

Elliot, S.N., Kratochwill, T.R., & Littlefield, J.F. (2000). *Education psychology*. Madison: Brown & Benchmark.

Suggested Web sites

Educational Psychology Interactive
 http://chiron.valdosta.edu.whuitt/edpsyint.html
Theory into Practice Database
 http://tip.psychology.org/index.html
The Jean Piaget Society
 http://www.piaget.org
Southeastern Center for the Enhancement of Learning
 http://www.scel.org/feuerstein.htm
Vygotsky Resources
 http://www.kolar.org/vygotsky
Albert Bandura
 http://www.psy.pdx.edu/PsiCafe/KeyTheorists/Bandura.htm
Robert Sternberg's personal homepage from Yale University
 http://www.yale.edu/rjsternberg/index.html
 http://www.yale.edu/pace/teammembers/personalpages/bob.html
David Ausubel
 http://ivc.uidaho.edu/mod/models/ausubel/index.html
Howard Gardner
 http://pzweb.harvard.edu/Pls/HG.htm

Table 7.5 Tutor's guide for PBL tutorial 1

Tutorial session	Learning stage	Learners' activities	Learners' deliverables	PBL tutor's role
PBL tutorial 1 (2 hours)	Problem encounter Induction into collaborative learning Problem clarification	Developing collegiality Individual reading, reflection and inquiry Commitment to team roles and to group Brainstorming and articulation of probable issues Consensus on problem statement Commitment to deliberate on problem scenario and problem analysis Induction into self-directed learning	Forging professionalism and friendship Notes or mind map of discussion Journal of problem statement	Develop an environment of learning, sharing, collegiality and professionalism through appropriate ice-breaking activities Present problem situation Facilitate communication, problem inquiry, clarification, identification, definition and delimitation
Self-directed learning (1 hour)	Deliberation of problem scenario and statement Initiation of problem analysis			

Table 7.6 Tutor's guide for PBL tutorial 2

Tutorial session	Learning stage	Learners' activities	Learners' deliverables	PBL tutor's role
PBL tutorial 2 (2 hours)	Problem analysis and learning issues	Brainstorming and analysis of problem (e.g. generation of possible explanations, hypotheses, etc.)	Journal of problem inquiry	Facilitate and guide identification of key learning objectives
			List of inquiries, explanations, ideas and hypotheses	Ensure learning and ownership of learning objectives
		Identification of learning issues and formulation of learning objectives	Statement of learning issues and objectives	Provide guidance on possible sources of information for reading and research
		Assignment of self-directed learning and peer teaching	Statement of learning contract on self-directed learning and peer teaching roles	
Self-directed learning (4–6 hours)	Identification of sources of information; reading, studying and research with a view to offering informed explanation for the problem and teaching peers on topic			
	Preparation of pointers and notes for sharing and teaching			

Table 7.7 Tutor's guide for PBL tutorials 3 and 4

Tutorial session	Learning stage	Learners' activities	Learners' deliverables	PBL tutor's role
PBL tutorial 3 (2 hours)	Discovery and reporting	Report on self-directed learning Peer teaching	Evidence of integration and consolidation of information as a group and as individuals Statement on sources of learning, information and research	Probe and question to facilitate learning of key concepts, principles and theories Provide comprehensive and critical evaluation and statement of research resources
Self-directed learning (4–6 hours)	Further self-study and research			
PBL tutorial 4 (2 hours)	Preparation of solution presentation	Synthesis of findings for presentation	Write-ups and reports	Facilitate connection and communication of information Ensure good research and deep learning
Self-directed learning (4–6 hours)	Synthesis of learning Review and evaluation of solution			

Table 7.8 Tutor's guide for PBL tutorials 5 and 6

Tutorial session	Learning stage	Learners' activities	Learners' deliverables	PBL tutor's role
PBL tutorial 5 (2 hours)	Solution presentation and reflection	Group presentation of findings Learning from other groups	Presentation package	Facilitate and assess quality of independent and group work
Self-directed learning (6 hours)	Compilation of group report, portfolio and essay			
PBL tutorial 6 (2 hours)	Presentation, overview and evaluation	Continuation of group presentation of findings Group evaluation of process and learning experience Summary and integration	Learning portfolios, reports of group and individual reviews and evaluations	Facilitate and assess quality of independent and group evaluation Summarize key learning theories

Jerry, Seow Jing and Pakti have been good friends since they met two years ago at a charity function. It all started with some ice-breaking activities at that function and they discovered that they have something in common – they like to work with people. Jerry had been working as a bank executive for two years until recently. His bank was reorganized and he volunteered to leave to take up a new job. He has just joined the teaching profession. Prior to his banking job, he had taught as an "untrained" teacher for six months at a neighbourhood secondary school. Seow Jing graduated from a local university and has been working as a relief teacher at a government-aided primary school for about two months to "test" if she would really enjoy teaching. Pakti graduated from an overseas university and is planning to join the teaching profession. He has been relief-teaching at an independent school. In a recent get-together, they got into talking about their experiences with students.

"The other week I had to teach a primary 4 class and I was supposed to teach them problems on volume. I really didn't know how I should do it, so I just gave them the formula $L \times B \times H$. However, I think many of them didn't understand," Seow Jing began.

"You should have brought a rectangular tank, poured some water in it and shown them a real example," Pakti suggested.

"You're right. Then there was this word problem that even I took quite a while to understand, and they're supposed to learn that," lamented Seow Jing.

"Nowadays, I think you're expected to add and multiply even at primary 1. I don't remember having to do that when I was six years old," said Pakti.

"Sometimes I wonder if kids are ready to learn these things at that age. There must be certain ages when children are ready to learn something," added Seow Jing.

"You know, I find that it's not easy to teach even secondary 1 students abstract concepts," Pakti added.

"How do children and adolescents acquire concepts?" asked Seow Jing.

"Think of your own experience – how did you learn in school?" offered Jerry.

"I can't really remember, but I think people around me – my older brothers, parents and teachers – played a big role," responded Seow Jing.

Pakti added, "For me, I think it was discussing with my classmates that helped."

Figure 7.5 Problem scenario 1 in educational psychology

Alfonso, Celina and Toon have just returned from two weeks of school attachment. They are sharing their classroom observations and experiences.

Alfonso says, "I observed several English and mathematics lessons for secondary 3 normal-stream students. Often the students did not seem to remember what had been taught in the previous lessons and were very restless. It seems to me that most of the teaching was one way, with students listening passively and inattentively. A few of the students looked distracted and seemed to be preoccupied with other things."

According to Alfonso, when he suggested to the teacher about using activities, the teacher's response was that "all these theories about learning and activities don't work in our situations". Alfonso says, "I am not sure what theories she was referring to, but surely there must be better ways to help these students learn."

Toon has this to share: "I had the opportunity to observe lower and upper secondary students in the normal stream. There was this teacher who taught chemistry and biology in a secondary 3 class. He seemed to use a drill-and-practice method rather successfully. He was very organized. What he did was to have a few objectives clearly stated before he explained the content. He then gave a number of short fill-in-the-blank questions. When the students completed the exercise, he would have them check each other's work in pairs as he went through the answers. At the end of each lesson, he seemed to give the students a sense of achievement in that they had at least mastered a few concepts. He would then give them some short questions as homework. Come the next lesson, he would start with the homework questions and then built on what had been taught. His method appeared to help students master the basic vocabulary, concepts and principles pretty well."

"My students were express-stream and gifted students," Celina says. "I was observing the students and I found that they were all very different in the ways they learnt. Some of them liked to ask a lot of questions, which could be disruptive; some worked well in pairs and group work; and others seemed to daydream but had no problem understanding when quizzed. I don't think the drill-and-practice approach will be helpful for the students I observed – they need much more challenging questions and tasks; otherwise they'd switch off. So it is very important to know how to stimulate these young minds."

"So how do we know how to cater to different students and help them learn?" Alfonso asks. "Experience, I suppose," Toon replies.

"Ya, but someone said, even if you have taught for ten years, it may be just ten years of the same experience rather than ten years of solid experience!" responds Alfonso, somewhat exasperated.

"Wise men learn from experience, but wiser men learn from the experience of others – that's what my university professor used to say!" exclaims Celina.

Figure 7.6 Problem scenario 2 in educational psychology

Problem statement

Read thoroughly the problem scenario. Give yourself time to think and try to contextualize the problem in the light of your prior knowledge and experience.

The purpose of the problem scenario is twofold:

1. To trigger learning of the skills, knowledge and attitudes needed to address such educational challenges
2. To learn about the process of acquiring such knowledge and about the process of making informed decisions as a reflective practitioner

You are required to come up with a problem statement in your own words. You should work on the problem individually, pen your own thoughts and deliberate it as a group. As in real-life situations, the information given is never quite complete. You may want to clarify terms, concepts and assumptions. You are required to brainstorm and come to a consensus on a problem statement to be submitted as a group. To develop the problem statement, the group should attempt to understand the problem by asking questions such as these: What is the situation in need of improvement? What is the nature of the problem? What is your commitment to finding out plausible solutions?

Problem inquiry and analysis

You are to submit your group inquiries and analyses. You may list them as pointers and questions. You may use tabulation and various templates, such as a listing of situation and hypothesis. Do not be judgemental when the group is coming up with ideas. At this stage, you would be activating your prior knowledge or experience and addressing possible explanations and hypotheses. Allow a free flow of ideas and only prioritize and select at the later stage. If possible, you should also come up with a map (e.g. mind map, concept map, block diagram) as a conceptual framework for generating your "solutions".

Learning issues and goals

Following your inquiry and analysis, you would want to confirm or reject explanations and hypotheses and address learning gaps. At this stage, the group will list learning needs and identify learning issues. This crucial stage of the problem-based learning process is when you state key learning issues and objectives (i.e. what is important for you to know). The group should formulate a list of learning objectives and issues. These may be stated in the form of questions. When that is done, the group will assign learning tasks for self-directed learning and peer teaching.

Figure 7.7 Sample of student's guide (truncated)

Table 7.9 Example of PBL assessment criteria for an educational psychology course

Component	Learning	Documents/Processes	Assessment	Marks
Problem and learning issues (10 marks)	Problem encounter and development of learning objectives	Problem statement	Clarity and definition of problem	5
		List of inquiries and generation of hypotheses	Thinking skills as evident by quantity and quality of ideas and hypotheses	5
		Formulation of learning objectives	Comprehensiveness and quality of learning objectives	5
Group work (20 marks)	Reporting, peer teaching, group presentation	Reporting and peer teaching	Peer evaluation	5
		Group presentation	Quality of solution (ideas and research) and presentation	15
Learning to learn (30 marks)	Writing of portfolio and reflective essay	Individual portfolio: your learning and learning from others (1,500–2,000 words)	Integration of group report and individual work. Quality of synthesis. Reflection and critical evaluation of self-directed learning. Quality of resources and team learning	10
		Reflection on learning and the learner (2,500–3,000 words)	Critical reflection and understanding of learning and the learner. Articulation of solution and personal view and belief underpinned by informed knowledge, theories and contextualization	20
Total	Overall			60

Table 7.10 Sample peer evaluation form

Name of group member			
Attitude (positiveness and helpfulness)	2 4 6 8 10	2 4 6 8 10	2 4 6 8 10
Participation (commitment and sharing)	2 4 6 8 10	2 4 6 8 10	2 4 6 8 10
Communication (clarity and sensitivity)	2 4 6 8 10	2 4 6 8 10	2 4 6 8 10
Enthusiasm (motivate self and others)	2 4 6 8 10	2 4 6 8 10	2 4 6 8 10
Resourcefulness (quality and comprehensiveness of contribution)	2 4 6 8 10	2 4 6 8 10	2 4 6 8 10
Total			

Health-care Course Unit

The following is a problem used in a health-care course unit on communicating with elderly patients.

> *This is a journal entry of Florence, a health-care worker.*
>
> *The door was ajar. I knocked on the door. There was a lady sitting in her wheelchair gazing out of the window. Since there was no answer, I decided to knock again. This time I asked, "Would you like to have a visitor today?" Still there was no answer. I thought to myself, "Maybe she cannot hear me." As I walked into her room, she saw me and reached out to me. I took her cold hands and placed them both in the warmth of mine. I introduced myself in the hope of receiving her response. As I continued trying to communicate, I spoke into her ear, but there was no response. So I kneeled at her side and held her hands. Finally, I decided it was time for me to go. As I stood up beside her to leave, I said, "My dear friend, I have to go for now. I will be back to see you again one day soon." While I leaned over and gently hugged her, she held onto me for a brief moment. I walked towards the door, and all of a sudden there was a wailing yell from inside the room. I turned around to face the elderly woman and she sweetly looked up at me. There was no one else in this room except her and me. As I walked over to her this time, I expected her to speak aloud. She looked at me, reached out her hand and still did not speak.*
>
> *Suppose you were in Florence's shoes, what would you do to communicate with the elderly lady?*

The learning goals in this PBL unit include content knowledge about interpersonal communication with the elderly, structured reflection to gain an enhanced insight into professional practice and development of therapeutic relationship with the elderly, problem-solving skills pertaining to analysis of behaviours and ways of managing functional behaviours, and lifewide skills of teamwork and information mining.

The learning issues of this problem can be:

- Learning issue 1: How can communication with the elderly be facilitated by active listening, hearing, verbalizing and visualizing verbal and non-verbal messages?
- Learning issue 2: How does aging and diseases affect communication?
- Learning issue 3: In what ways can one succeed in communicating effectively with the elderly?

The PBL cycle takes the unit through seven two-hour sessions as shown in Table 7.11.

Table 7.11 PBL cycle in a health-care course unit

Session	Activities
Tutorial 1 PBL induction (pre-PBL session)	Developing PBL environment: brief students on expectations of PBL and on independent and group learning
	Preparing students' mindset for learning through problems, reflective thinking, online communication using discussion board with lecturer and group members
	Preparing students to work as a team: explain roles of individual group members, specific roles and communication channels
Tutorial 2 Problem encounter	Learner's activities: understand and agree on what the problem is; delineate boundaries of the problem; clarify scenario and assumptions
Tutorial 3 Problem analysis and learning issues	Brainstorming and analysis of problem: decide on approaches to solve the problem; present possible explanations and statement of hypotheses; identify learning issues, formulate learning objectives
Tutorial 4 Peer teaching and solution presentation of learning issue 1 Tutorial 5 Peer teaching and solution presentation of learning issue 2 Tutorial 6 Peer teaching and solution presentation of learning issue 3	Reporting on self-directed learning and peer teaching: group members take turns to present the information and share the research resources; group integrates and synthesizes the information, and assesses information gathered in terms of quality and comprehensiveness of coverage Group presentation, role play and demonstrations to illustrate solution and findings; questions and answers from other groups
Tutorial 7 Closure and synthesis	Lecturer presents overview and critique Groups evaluate their learning experiences

Law Subjects

Here we shall see how the goals of PBL illustrated in Figure 6.1 are incorporated in law subjects. The PBL goals of this problem are as follows:

- To acquire content and professional knowledge pertaining to the law of real property and to company law
- To develop problem-solving skills in real-world business situations
- To develop independent learning skills
- To learn collaboration skills, teamwork and effective inter-dependence

The problem is designed as a sequel to an earlier problem on setting up a company and the purchase and lease of a property. The problems are designed to cater for cross-disciplinary learning in at least two subjects: property law and company law. This problem is meant to teach the application of the property and company laws to the construction/property business. The following is the problem scenario.

You are working in a legal firm and have been assigned to interview the clients Mr Neta and Ms Flora. Your boss has asked you to draft a legal opinion to address the concerns of these clients. The following is the information given by the clients.

Mr Neta:

My business partners, Flora and Dino, are giving me problems. They have decided to convert our tea business into a spa business without consulting me. They held an informal tea party last week and made that decision, even though I objected. They conducted an informal vote by a show of hands, which I feel is improper for such an important decision. I am only one shareholder against the two of them, so I was outvoted. What can I do? They also mentioned something about IPO [initial public offering] and thinking "big". I'm not very educated; I don't know what the big deal is about IPO.

Ms Flora:

Our company has decided to buy a piece of land in the business district to build a high-rise commercial building. We will sell the top floors and keep the ground floor for our new spa business. We've never built any high-rise buildings before, so I'm not sure what legal issues we need to look at. One thing I'm concerned with is how we will divide the title of the land among all the buyers. I understand that we must be careful to ensure that the buyers do not change the "external look" of our building on their own without our consent as it will affect the value of our property. We must find some way to control the buyers' renovation plans. One of our partners, Mr Neta, is giving us trouble – he is against the purchase of any type of land except freehold. He found out that the land we are buying is an "estate in perpetuity" and is kicking up a big fuss over it. I told him that it is the same as freehold, but he is not convinced.

Problems can be presented through role play, besides as textual information. At Temasek Polytechnic, where PBL has been used creatively in its law courses, tutors actually role-play as the clients. In that way, students learn interviewing skills, and these competencies too could be assessed by the tutors.

The learning issues in such a problem can be:

On company law:

- What is the procedure for changing the nature of a company's business?
- How do clients amend object clauses?
- What are the proper procedures in a meeting? What is voting by hand and by poll? Were there any irregularities in the shareholders' meeting?
- What are Mr Neta's rights as a minority shareholder? Can he take action if his views are disregarded?
- Is it worthwhile for the company to be listed? What is an IPO? What are the advantages of an IPO?

On the law of real property:

- How does a company go about developing a high-rise commercial building? What are the steps they have to take?
- How does a company transfer title to each individual purchaser when the units are sold?
- How can a company ensure that all purchasers (present and future) abide by the restriction of not altering the external look of their unit?
- Is an estate in perpetuity also a freehold property? How are they different?

In this case, a six-week PBL cycle is used, as shown in Table 7.12.

Table 7.12 PBL cycle for teaching law subjects

Week	PBL stage	Activities
Week 1	Meet the problem	Students interview "clients" to obtain information for the problem. They also get together in their groups to set the ground rules for the group's functioning.
Week 2	Problem analysis	Using a template of Facts–Ideas–Issues–Action, students organize the information and decide what extra information is needed or what assumptions they have to make. They put their questions in the Action column and then post them online for discussion.
Week 3	Generating ideas and learning issues	Students generate ideas on how to solve the problem and decide on the topics they need to read up in order to come up with their learning issues. At this point, they may split up the research work. Students will then do preliminary research and reading and formulate their learning issues. They will discuss the issues with the facilitator, who will help them refine the issues.
Week 4	Discovery and reporting	Armed with the issues, students will do detailed research on the laws relating to the concerns of their clients. At this point, the facilitator will do a resource critique with students. Students will then share their findings and undertake peer teaching with their group members.
Week 5	Solution presentation	After some discussions on how the laws can be applied to their clients' cases, students will draft their individual written legal opinion to be handed in to their "boss". The opinion will contain the learning issues as well as the researched laws and their application, the conclusion and recommendations for the cases.
Week 6	Reflection and consolidation of learning	Students will reflect on their problem-solving process and how they have performed as a team player. They will look at the ground rules set earlier by the group and evaluate their own performance as a problem solver and as a team member as well as their adherence to the ground rules. This will be done in an open feedback session with their facilitator, where team members will also give each other feedback on their performance in these areas. The facilitator will assess their ability to self-evaluate and to give and receive feedback. There will also be a session for consolidation of learning where the facilitator will go through the answers for the problem and teach the content using mind maps drawn by students of the various topics of the subjects. This will close the loop of learning.

At the end of the six weeks, in addition to the written legal opinion and feedback appraisal, students have to submit a portfolio of write-ups and notes as evidence of the progress and development of their learning from week 1 to week 6.

Design Course

Design courses provide many opportunities and scope for infusing PBL. Giving students real-world design problems is an excellent way to trigger learning. Consider the following problem for an interior design course, where one of the modules is on materials.

A 50-year-old hotel near a beach has been newly renovated. The floor was previously covered with vinyl, but following the renovation carpets were laid on every level of the building. A few months after the renovation, the hotel owner observed discoloration of the carpet. The situation was worse in the basement. Thinking that it could be due to the inferiority of the carpets, he decided to change to a more expensive range. After spending more money, he discovered to his horror that the problem persisted. He could not understand why this happened when

Table 7.13 PBL cycle for an interior design module

PBL stage	Purpose and activities
PBL introduction	To ensure all members participate actively and to encourage open discussions, set the climate of learning and roles. Brief on process and procedures of the groups. Explain desired learning outcomes: acquisition of problem-solving skills, teamwork skills and new knowledge.
Problem identification	Students deliberate on problem and identify key issues, such as: • Why did the carpets discolour after only a few months? • Why was the problem particularly bad at the basement? • Why did changing the carpets to a more expensive range fail to solve the problem? • Why has that problem not occur at another hotel some distance away?
Brainstorming and idea generation	Analyse the problems identified and give possible explanations, such as: • Not all carpets are the same.

	• The location of the hotel (next to the beach) exposes it to moisture with a high salt content, which may have created the problem. • Basements are more difficult to maintain than other levels. • Carpets may need to be specially installed in wetness-prone areas. • Price has little relevance to the appropriateness of carpet types.
Learning issues	Identify the learning issues from the hypothesis, such as: • To understand the properties of carpets • To understand how carpets are classified • To understand how the quality of carpet is determined • To understand how carpets are installed (particularly in wetness-prone areas such as basements) • To understand problems related to the use of carpets • To understand the use of carpets in relation to environmental conditions
Self-directed learning	Students select the learning issues that interest them most or in which they lack the knowledge. Strategies of learning include: • finding relevant information from journals, textbooks or online databases • talking to experts, such as carpet suppliers and contractors • interviewing carpet users
Peer teaching and "expert roles"	Having gathered the information, students assume the role of "expert" for the topic they explored and present their findings.
Synthesis and application	Groups summarize, integrate and evaluate information for validity and relevance. They also review the credibility and appropriateness of the resources. The knowledge gained is applied and the solution developed.
Reflection and feedback	The final stage is to review and evaluate what has been learnt: principles, concepts and applications. Students also reflect on the problem-solving process, the best ways of learning and the professional knowledge gained.

another hotel located further down the road has been using carpets as floor coverings for the last few years without any problem.

The problem in this case is used over four to five tutorial sessions with a PBL cycle as shown in Table 7.13.

Although the problem stimulus in this case may be a simple scenario, the cycle can take longer depending on the emphasis of the PBL goals. Assessment can be based on journal reports, management of research, teamwork, peer evaluation, presentation skills and the final presentation of recommendations and solutions.

Service Skills

PBL is also used in many cases to acquire valuable learning skills where the curriculum goals may not include very well-defined disciplinary knowledge. Suppose a high school or secondary school is interested in teaching their student leaders planning skills related to service provision or general project management. The following problem scenario may suffice as a trigger:

Mr Lee Dushi, a teacher at a secondary school in Singapore, is organizing an overseas trip for 40 students. The purpose of the trip is to give students greater exposure to life outside their "comfort zone" and to prepare them for service and challenges in an increasingly global world. An international foundation has agreed to sponsor the trip and proposed that they go to a village in Giay in the vicinity of Hanoi. They are to help with the finishing touches (painting, fixing of doors, etc.) of a small school building that is near completion. They will be there for two full weeks. Dushi has never organized an overseas trip before. You and a few others who are going on the trip have been tasked to help with the preparations for the trip.

The goals of this PBL exercise may include helping students learn:

- the logistics of planning for an overseas trip
- research and information-mining techniques
- problem-solving skills
- teamwork skills
- presentation skills

The PBL programme and the time frame may be organized as follows:

- Meet the problem and analysis of the problem   2 hours
- Self-directed learning   4 hours
- Sharing and synthesis   4 hours
- Presentation of solution   2 hours
- Feedback and evaluation   1 hour

A KND template may be suggested and students are told to prepare a presentation of their proposals for helping to organize the trip. They may be required to write a report to announce the trip with a description of the place they are going and highlighting the service to be rendered.

In the first session, students would read the problem and seek to understand what is involved and try to use the template. They are expected to draw up the lists of issues related to this problem, as in Table 7.14.

For self-directed learning, sharing and synthesis, students will do research or seek information based on the "to do" list.

The final presentation will be on each group's plan on how to make the trip successful. Students may be assessed on their teamwork and the quality of the presentation.

Table 7.14 Example of a KND template for the service problem scenario

What we know	What we need to know	To do
• Objectives of the trip: exposure to life overseas outside our comfort zone; to be prepared for service	• Geography and climate of Giay	• Form committees for various tasks (logistics, programme, etc.)
• Task: to help painting and simple carpentry work	• Culture of Vietnamese	• Draw up a work plan
• Who is going and how many: 40 students	• Involvement of tour agent and transportation arrangements	• Draw up the budget
• Destination: Giay near Hanoi	• Accommodation arrangements	• Learn about geography of the place
• Duration of stay: two weeks	• Contact person in Giay	• Learn about the culture
• Sponsor: an international foundation	• Programme for the task/project	• Learn some basic Vietnamese language
• Teacher in charge: Lee Dushi (no experience)	• Plans of the school building	• Draw up a schedule of pre-trip tasks
	• Facilities available in Giay	• Hold a training workshop on painting and carpentry
	• Equipment we may need	• Learn about community service
	• Budget/Costs	• Prepare the two-week programme and itinerary
	• Any need to raise funds and from where	
	• Manpower: other teachers	
	• Visa/Passport matters	
	• Guidelines for students on overseas trip	
	• Issues of parental consent	
	• Insurance issues	
	• Health and safety issues	

8

PROBLEM-BASED LEARNING AND E-LEARNING

Developments in Internet Communication Technology

A discourse on PBL as an educational innovation would not be complete without a discussion on e-learning. Chen and Tan (2002) observed that we are bombarded by reports of rapid and constant changes in Internet communication technologies (ICT). There have also been ample claims of breakthrough technologies and promises of new ways of learning and a new generation of learners. The power of ICT in terms of communication and information accessibility (e.g. e-mail, World Wide Web, Internet telecommunications, video-conferencing) is obvious. I mentioned in Chapter 1 that the information age makes the traditional means of information dissemination obsolete. However, if teaching continues to be primarily teacher-directed and didactic, there is little need for students to go to the Internet for information. Problems given only after the knowledge has been disseminated through lectures do not optimize on the availability of and the accessibility to information.

The use of PBL empowers students to not only take advantage of the accessibility as well as the wealth of knowledge but also to discover the means of knowledge sharing, knowledge propagation and knowledge enterprise through the use of learning management systems, Web-based learning and Internet communication.

PBL and Learning Management Systems

The nature of PBL and PBL processes provide ample opportunities for PBL curricula to make full use of learning management systems available to educational institutions today. Learning management systems like WebCT, Topclass and Blackboard provide excellent tools for the dissemination of problem scenarios, accessing online resources and linkages to Web sites, and for group discussions. For example, in the educational psychology PBL unit described in the previous chapter, all problem scenarios and course details are presented through the Blackboard platform for students to access.

Since PBL requires a mindset change in students that calls for initiative, ownership and independence, such online learning management systems are fitting for facilitating the learning process. Although PBL is totally student-centred, PBL tutors' role is critical in developing the environment of learning and helping to facilitate communication, problem inquiry, critical evaluation and metacognition. In PBL, students are encouraged to hold discussions beyond the tutorial sessions. Apart from face-to-face communication, many-to-many discussions and chats are possible through online learning platforms. Figure 8.1 illustrates how a learning management system facilitates the PBL process.

Currently, many learning management systems, such as Blackboard, provide convenient tools and resources, such as announcements, course information, course documents, assignments, books, communication system, virtual classroom and discussion board. With rapid improvement, the tools and sequencing are becoming more flexible and user-friendly. This means that we will be able to customize the learning management system to suit a particular PBL programme. Furthermore, problems can be easily presented in a variety of innovative ways, including text, hypertext, photographs, graphics and digital videos. A rich amount of data, Web sites and Internet links can also be conveniently incorporated.

To facilitate the PBL process, we suggest making the following information and resources available online 24 hours:

- PBL homepage
- Course objectives
- Course structure
- Portfolio of problem scenarios
- PBL cycle and inquiry tools
- Tutor's guide
- Student's guide
- Resources and links
- Assessment criteria
- Communication system

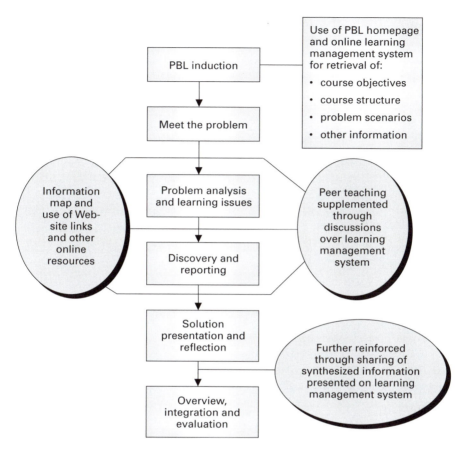

Figure 8.1 Usage of learning management system in the PBL process

The opportunities for PBL and e-learning integration abound considering what learning management systems and Web-based learning could offer. Since PBL involves immersion in the problem as well as the collection, connection and communication of information over an extended period of time, such learning management systems will support and facilitate the learning and communication process.

The effective integration of PBL models and e-learning appears to be a promising way to go in educational and training innovation. The creative combination of face-to-face mediation and technological mediation will characterize learning in the future. It would be unwise for educators to ignore the use of problems and the psychological and motivational benefits of PBL processes. In PBL, face-to-face interaction is important for learning the complexities and heuristics of thinking, problem solving and application through inquiry and discussion. It is difficult to structure and sequence such metacognitive learning. Perhaps artificial intelligence and more sophisticated multimedia delivery and interaction will assist in more domains of metacognitive learning in the future.

Innovating e-Learning

Whilst a blend of face-to-face teaching and the use of technology is preferred, there are many instances where circumstances call for human–machine interaction as a primary mode of learning. Making e-learning work has, however, been a challenge. Not too long ago, e-learning business was one of the gold rushes during the dotcom fever. High return on investment in e-learning was predicted, but, as Welber (2002) noted, nearly all the e-learning companies have yet to make a profit. Many online providers are struggling with the design of interactivity. Many universities and online companies have invested heavily in their attempts to harness the power of technology in instructional design with a view to launching commercially viable e-learning programmes. Some institutions like the Massachusetts Institute of Technology (MIT) decided instead that they would simply provide free resources. In April 2001 MIT announced its OCW (OpenCourseWare) and promised to put a comprehensive range of its professors' course material for free access to the world. A good range of content is now available on the MIT Web site (http://ocw.mit.edu). The institute made it clear that it was not generally making available its courses for interaction; OCW is in no way close to an MIT education. For MIT, education is face-to-face interaction with lecturers, sharing their knowledge, expertise and inspirational personal qualities.

However, we still need to make e-learning work because it is useful in situations where there are geographical and time constraints, as in distance learning, learning from remote sites and just-in-time training. There are also circumstances such as the recent SARS (severe acute respiratory syndrome) epidemic when educational institutions in certain affected countries were ordered to close for several weeks. A professor from a university in Hong Kong told me that they had to consider seriously the use of e-learning as an alternative and complement.

One serious consideration for e-learning programme providers is to take the PBL approach and make the best of technology to facilitate the collaborative and problem-solving learning processes. By using problems as triggers for learning and interactivity, the potential of technology could perhaps be more fully harnessed. Table 8.1 summarizes the paradigm shift when we move from current e-learning practices to the use of PBL in e-learning.

Some of the underpinning principles of the use of PBL in e-learning are:

> The best instructional strategy for e-learning is to use problems as triggers of learning. The e-learning environment is perfect for PBL cycles. PBL approaches provide the motivation for online learning engagement in terms of connecting to resources, peers and experts.

- Make use of the power of real-world problems to motivate learning
- Design the learning environment such that it employs the global information network
- Encourage the development of learning-to-learn processes, heuristics, and thinking skills
- Emphasize problem solving and decision making rather than content learning
- Provide for systems of engagement and collaboration
- Provide opportunities for active application of knowledge and self-review
- Optimize the use of flexible structures to support and sustain independence and interdependence
- Develop evaluative and critical use of information sources

Table 8.1 Using PBL in e-learning

Current e-learning	PBL e-learning
Changes mode of delivery	Changes paradigm of learning
Passive definition of scope	Active definition of scope
Retrieval of content	Learning of process
Primarily linear structuring of content	Scaffolding of thinking
Little activation of prior knowledge	Activation of prior knowledge
Limited engagement	Inevitable engagement
Flexibility used	Flexibility optimized
Single discipline	Multiple disciplines
Primarily convergent	Encourages divergence
Communication mainly one–one	Communication one–many and many–many
Individual learning	Peer/Collaborative learning
Information search minimal	Information search extensive
Little evaluation of information sources	Emphasizes review and critique of information sources

9

STUDENTS' EXPERIENCES OF PROBLEM-BASED LEARNING

The Heart of PBL: Students' Learning

I had observed in my research on how lecturers designed curricula that little attention was given to the needs of learners and to what learners would be empowered to do (Tan, 1994). Using the models of Oliva (1992) and Diamond (1989) on considerations (hence time invested in planning) given to (1) the learner, (2) the society, and (3) the subject matter, I found in my survey of academic staff that only 27 per cent of them gave high ratings for considering the learner as the most important focus. In contrast, 65.4 per cent rated highly consideration given to the subject matter. In other words, staff tended to be preoccupied with what they taught and would invest a large part of their energies, deliberations and concern on issues of content knowledge. These findings are consistent with Ramsden's (1998) view that the needs of learners and how they would learn have not been given sufficient attention. In PBL, however, the students as active learners and problem solvers form the heart of the PBL experience.

In this chapter, I will share gleanings from case vignettes of students. What are students saying about PBL? I think the very people who are the focus of PBL can help us gain insights into how PBL empowers them or perhaps creates helplessness. Are students finding more meaning or clearer direction with PBL or are they perhaps more lost? Does PBL meet students' needs? What are their perceptions and experiences of PBL? The students in these vignettes were from different populations: postgraduate, university and polytechnic students who experienced PBL for the first time. We shall look at their experiences in terms of their interaction with problems, collaborative learning, problem solving, self-directed learning and the coaching process.

Problems: Do They Frustrate or Empower?

Student A1

I really received a culture shock. PBL was definitely not my style of learning. I was really frustrated that no teachers would give out notes or provide information in a well-structured and systematic manner. It seemed to lack proper direction and structure and I was lost. At the end no "model" answers were provided.

Student A2

Doing PBL is like solving a jigsaw puzzle. It is frustrating because we were not given any big picture, not even the scope, at the beginning. The problem is like giving us a few jigsaw pieces and asking us to find the rest of the pieces. The worst thing is that at the end of everything I still don't get an overall picture.

Student A3

There are too many learning issues. We don't have the foundation knowledge. There are just too many things left for us to find out on our own and we just can't cope. We don't even know where to begin. My group lost interest because of PBL. There were times when the tutor sent us on a wild goose chase.

Student A4

I think the problems were very helpful because they kept us focused on thinking about the learning issues and the solutions. Even when we were not using the library or checking the Net, we continued to think about them.

Student A5

In the course, we were given real-world problems and we really wanted to work on them because we knew they are the kinds of things we would face in the future. For example, we had this problem where we were told about a tank made of a certain material that was part of a system in an industrial plant. When the tank was used with concentrated nitric acid, everything worked fine. But one day someone used that same tank with a more diluted form of nitric acid. After some time the tank began to leak. Why did reducing the acid concentration seem to lead to leakage? We were told it was a real case and we were very curious to find out why. There were many learning issues about the properties of the kinds of metal and materials used for making tanks. This problem really required a lot of knowledge on materials. We also learnt a great deal about acids used in industry. I can say that although this problem was done many months ago I can remember most of what I had learnt.

Student A6

At the debrief, we had already submitted our solutions, but everybody, even the worst students, turned up. We had a guy who was probably one of the least committed and laziest students. Even he came. That's because all of us had spent a tremendous amount of time on the problem and we were really curious about the solution by this time. The lecturer revealed to us the various solution scenarios and emphasized that, although in this case there appeared to be an optimal or best solution, alternative solutions were possible.

In any PBL implementation, we will come across people like student A1, who finds that PBL is contrary to his or her learning style and continues to hope for spoon-feeding at some point in time. That is why we emphasize mindset change. Students A2 and A3 seem to have problem coping owing to their need for closer guidance and lack of foundation knowledge.

The power of a real-world problem is obvious from vignettes A4 and A5. I observe, however, that the power of problems has not been optimized in many PBL courses. The experience of student A5 indicates that students can appreciate the value of real-world problems from industry.

Collaborative Learning: Does It Work?

Student B1

Through the PBL process, I realized that I had always treated with disdain the various attempts to inculcate problem-solving skills (from secondary school to university). I never felt that these skills would benefit me in any way. However, in this course, I discovered the importance of being innovative and how, through PBL, creative thinking could be fostered. I realized that I needed to change my mindset, thus the whole experience was really a paradigm shift for me. I was thoroughly motivated by the fact that I no longer gathered information and solutions merely from textbooks or from my tutors. It was through the sessions of collaborative learning that I discovered this.

Student B2

Carrying out discussions and solving the various problem scenarios as a group improved my own learning process. This collaborative learning approach has helped me learn with and from others.

Student B3

My classmates came out with summaries of various chapters of the textbook and provided a brief overview for those who had not read those chapters. I found this quite effective and convenient.

Student B4

I am just a very average student and I find that I am sometimes very slow in understanding lecture-type courses. Once I can't follow, I get more and more lost. In PBL, however, I can learn at my own pace. I can tell my group members that I don't get it and they will explain it to me. Sometimes I really try hard to read, but I still cannot get it. The other members know my difficulty and will take time to explain to me.

Student B5

I think I receive a lot of benefit from PBL. There was this lecturer in a non-PBL subject; we really didn't know what he was teaching. But for the PBL subject, I really enjoy it because we read up and then share with each other. We speak in our own language. It's very different when we start talking to each other and check things out together, whereas by myself I sometimes cannot understand the stuff.

Student B6

I learn best on my own. I prefer a course where we are told what to study and I will spend my time working on it. I don't think PBL is better than the lecture method. If I read on my own, I can go into much more depth. Most of the sharing in PBL is superficial. It's not my style of learning.

Student B7

PBL requires us to work in groups and to find things out for ourselves, identify the learning issues and then teach each other. I have to say that I do not find the group learning helpful at all. All of us have very little knowledge of the subject. We don't have enough basic knowledge and we don't understand what we read.

How much time do we really have to read up? I'd rather have the lecturer explain things to us, instead of leaving us to struggle and learn nothing much even after the whole PBL unit is completed.

Student B8

Working in a group made me more aware of the constant dynamics a group faces. Through our discussions, I could see that at times there were instances of majority influence. There were some ideas that we did not all agree upon; but as long as three of us agreed on something, we tended to ignore the person who did not follow us.

Student B9

Even if there was only one person who did not play his or her part well, the whole group would suffer as we would not be well informed in that particular topic. As a result, we might have to spend additional time reading and researching on it. It would also be unfair as that person would just be benefiting from others' hard work.

Generally, most students find the collaborative approaches in PBL valuable, as indicated by vignettes B1 to B5. It appears to me, however, that more mature students (e.g. postgraduate students) tend to view collaborative learning in PBL more positively. This is not surprising since PBL approaches are often congruent with the principles of adult learning, where learners take responsibility for learning, share with others, set their learning goals and so on (Knowles, 1980). There are, however, students who resist the use of collaborative approaches. Other problems of group work include the issue of "majority" opinion, which may not always be right, and uncooperative group members.

I know of many schools and institutions that incorporated sessions on group dynamics and teamwork before they implement PBL, which may be a wise thing to do. Woods (2000) emphasized the importance of developing group-work skills and teamwork as prerequisites for students to really gain from the PBL experience. It is also important to build into assessment measures rewards for collaborative work. The use of peer assessment can also help deal with the problem of poor team learners. Most importantly, PBL tutors should be alert to the participation of students – this is why the class size in PBL should not be too large.

Problem Solving: Does It Lead to Learning?

Student C1

I am not sure if the problem I have identified is indeed the crux, or if it is merely peripheral. Worse still, what if I were dealing with the "wrong" problem, so to speak? In this sense, I still think the lecturer needs to feature prominently in the PBL approach.

Student C2

I think that the problem identification part is vital because it will determine if the learner sets off on the right footing or not. I guess one can treat this as part of the learning process, but I also worry about the possibility that I might be working on a "wrong" problem without realizing it until much later.

Student C3

Although I still have strong attachment to the drill-and-practice method, I must confess that PBL completely revolutionizes the way I think and solve problems. In fact, it enables me to look at a problem from different angles and come up with various solutions to it. Through PBL, I realized that there are many ways to solve a particular problem, as opposed to the traditional narrow view of having only a single solution to a given question or problem.

Student C4

Throughout the entire process, I realized that I was constantly thinking about the problem and reflecting on the solutions. Even though some of the problems seemed so trivial and simple on the surface, there were actually a much deeper explanation and a much more complicated process involved. The constant questioning and evaluation that went through my mind kept me thinking more deeply into the issues of the case study.

Student C5

I was pleasantly surprised. The amount and diversity of insights from my group mates, and the different arguments we had, made the discussion very stimulating. New viewpoints were generated when we put ourselves into the shoes of the characters in the problem scenarios. The realism of the issues made the process of problem solving more engaging and invigorating.

Student C6

To solve a problem was now not as simple as just finding a solution and leaving it at that, but coming up with different problem statements, generating learning issues and hypotheses, and thinking up questions. All these made the problem scenarios, in a sense, a little more three-dimensional. Some of the problem scenarios were quite long, so it helped me, personally, to divide the problems into smaller sections to make them easier to comprehend and solve.

Case vignettes C1 and C2 show a common experience of students: their uncertainty of the direction they are heading, particularly their identification of the problem and the learning issues. This points to the need for sufficient mediation by the tutor. As seen from vignettes C3 to C6, students are usually positive about the problem-solving experience in PBL. They are able to appreciate the value of the PBL cycle and experience, which enable them to gain diverse perspectives, apply different ways of thinking, and use reflection and metacognition.

Self-directed Learning: Is It Productive?

Student D1

I must say that PBL really helps me. I was on industrial attachment. The working environment is really different. You have to work with people you do not know. My trainer left me alone right from the first day. I was asked to do a number of things on my own without guidance, and I really felt very insecure because I had to operate the machine all by myself. I was forced to find things out. I think from the PBL experience I learnt to find things out, especially how to ask for information.

Student D2

I have learnt how to use the Net and the library to get information. Our tutors did not even give us any hints about key words. I found that key words are very important. If a key word doesn't work, we think of associated terms and so on. You have to think and make connections. This is a new skill I have learnt.

Student D3

We found that the Internet was very useful. We were fortunate in the sense that we had Internet connections in our homes, so most of our communication was done through the Internet. Sharing of findings could be done immediately as all we had to do was to forward to each other the interesting sites we found. The PowerPoint presentation was prepared mostly through e-mail, with the final touches done in school. We found it better to agree on formats and so on before meeting up in school to finish up the presentation.

Student D4

I tried to source for reading material from the library. There were so many books – which ones to choose? I had tried spending two afternoons going through the shelves to find suitable and interesting reading material. After reading two to three books, I was still unable to find my answers. Also, the books were rather technical, so I gave up.

Student D5

Internet search was unproductive for me. Much time was wasted clicking here and there. Although I did use some Internet information for our presentation, it was more copying and pasting information that I could understand. Heavy, technical stuff was not picked and analysed or used.

Student D6

For me to read and research, the material available (through any sources) has to be readable, that is, not too technical and is presented in an interesting manner. "Schematic" information helps – teachers could perhaps provide us this, especially for technical subjects.

Student D7

I think the biggest problem in PBL is that it requires a lot of time. We spent about a month discussing the same few problem scenarios. In order to go into details, we had to spend enough time so that we covered every aspect that we wanted to cover.

Many students, like D1, find that learning to seek information is a lifelong learning asset. Others like D2 and D3 also appreciate the importance of information mining and using the Internet. Vignettes D4 to D7 point out some of the common frustrations in independent learning. Firstly, students feel overwhelmed easily when left to seek for information without some guidelines. That is why when discussing curriculum development I included a resource guide as an essential item (see the example of an educational psychology course in

Chapter 7). Secondly, where the subject involves numerous technical definitions and concepts, students may need to be given the necessary foundation knowledge. For example, without the knowledge of calculus, it is unreasonable to expect students to understand the application of calculus in solving engineering problems. I am thus of the view that PBL should be used appropriately, especially with younger students.

Coaching Process: Does It Facilitate?

Student E1

I really enjoy PBL because we have a very understanding and caring tutor. She does not give us the answers, but she really listens and tries to understand where we are. I don't know about other groups, but our tutor really guides us in addressing the important issues. She is very good at probing and persuading us to want to find out more about the things important for solving the problems. Through her probing, she helps us see the many gaps, which cause us to reflect and think.

Student E2

In PBL, we really learn to think. We always use brainstorming sessions to come up with ideas. We also learn to distinguish facts from ideas. Through the tutor's prompting and questioning, we learn to ask good questions and to prioritize what is important after we have come up with possible ideas and issues. The tutor also taught us to use various thinking tools.

Student E3

I think through PBL we really have become better at problem solving. We learn to clarify our assumptions and concepts. We also ask more why-questions and apply logical, critical and creative thinking at various stages. I learn that one has to be flexible rather than become fixed with a particular mindset. Yes, I think the tutor plays an important role in helping us develop problem-solving skills in PBL.

Student E4

I think the tutors were told that they were not allowed to give us any hints or solutions, and this tutor really could not guide us. His famous statement was "So what do you think?" All that he could say was "What do you think?" Even when we were not asking for solutions or hints but some pointers to resources, his answer was "So what do you think?"!

Student E5

We were allowed to e-mail lecturers but mainly for appointments. Some staff allowed us to call them on the phone – even their handphone. However, each of us had timecards. The timecard allowed us to have 30 minutes of consultation or information feeding outside of the usual tutorial hours. We combined our timecard allotments to get a two-hour session. In that session, we tried to close all the gaps to our solutions.

Student E6

The PBL tutorial process doesn't work. We don't really like the tutor. She is very businesslike and assumes that we have all the time to work on the problem. We know that she is against spoon-feeding and that she has a good knowledge herself, but we hope she could understand what we are going through. She can give us more encouragement and guidance. Sometimes in our group discussion when we reach a critical point, all we need is just a little hint or something, or someone to tell us if we are going in the right direction; but we can only consult the tutor at specific times, and even then there seems to be a lot of things that we are not supposed to ask!

Student E7

I think it is OK if tutors don't want to give us answers straightaway, but I feel that the tutor should be prepared and be able to offer guidance when we need it. When we ask things about the problem, the tutor always says, "I don't know – you are supposed to find out" or "I don't know, what do you think?" In the first few tutorials, we thought he wanted to make us think, but after so many sessions we have come to the conclusion that the tutor really doesn't know. I think tutors should prepare and experience the problems themselves.

Student E8

Looking back, I think PBL could have worked better if the tutors had prepared us for it. We were very lost most of the time in the early stage, never knowing what to expect.

Student E9

For some of us, the groups did not work well because the tutor assumed that we would be able to start working with each other once we were assigned to the groups. The good tutors helped students get to know each other and took care to organize many activities that helped to develop class and group spirit.

These vignettes illustrate the experience, or at least the perceptions, of students in the PBL tutorial process and the quality of their interactions with tutors in PBL classrooms. In our experience, the lecturer as a coach is a major factor determining the effectiveness of PBL courses. The vignettes seem to raise some questions: What really is the role of the tutor? What are the characteristics of effective facilitators or coaches? What skills do tutors need to have to ensure that students benefit from the PBL process? How well are academic staff coaching and empowering students in the process?

The deduction drawn from this cluster of vignettes is that, whilst PBL is learner-centred, the role of the lecturer as facilitator is by no means passive. PBL does not just happen given a good problem, a well-designed schedule, relevant resources and the necessary opportunities for small group learning. The experiences of the students in this cluster support my view that staff development is necessary to equip tutors with PBL facilitation skills. Woods (2000) noted that one of the most challenging tasks in PBL is the development of process skills. He argued that both research and experience point to the fact that many process skills, such as change management, teamwork, conflict resolution and problem solving, do not just happen because students work in small groups. This calls for staff to be equipped with process skills (e.g. handling group dynamics, questioning, facilitating metacognition) and to be able to identify, articulate and assess these skills.

Conclusion

The case vignettes give us a better picture of what our students might be going through in PBL courses. They stress the need to prepare students, to design good problems and to develop PBL curricula carefully. Insights from these vignettes point to several important considerations, which are:

- to assess students' readiness in terms of foundation knowledge, maturity, needs and motivations

- to prepare students in terms of mindset change and skills for group work, reading, time management and information mining
- to plan for scaffolding processes in the PBL cycle
- to provide appropriate levels of resource guidance
- to design good and motivating problems
- to ensure that there is a closure process

I would like to point out that often not enough attention is given to ensure a good closure. Owing to the emphasis given to process, in most cases closure focuses on students sharing their reflections of how they perform as problem solvers and evaluation of their participation as team members. A neglected area is that of addressing how we look at the knowledge we have been dealing with in the PBL process (Berkson, 1993). As indicated in one of the vignettes, when students have been immersed in the problem for some time, they want to know how the story ends and hear the lecturer's synthesis. The observant tutor should take note of the convergence and divergence processes that students have experienced and should not only comment on the quality of review and synthesis but also provide his or her synthesis in the light of what students have done. As Schwartz and colleagues (2001) noted, it is important to demonstrate how divergent thinking and convergent thinking interact to produce an integrated solution. A good closure and debrief help provide confidence and affirmation of the particular heuristics that could be employed.

Whilst PBL appears promising in addressing individual differences in learning – the variety of learning styles and preferred modes of learning – we need to empathize with those whose learning styles and habits are less attuned to the PBL ways of learning. At the end of the PBL course, students generally feel more empowered in areas pertaining to independent learning, particularly the ability to retrieve information and to learn how to learn. Students' experiences also support PBL as a good approach for learning interdependence and socialization.

There appears to be a case for considering where and when it is best to implement PBL. Here I think there is a chasm between advocates of so-called "pure" or "authentic" PBL and the reality of students' experience. There are those who claim that PBL need not activate prior knowledge and that we could start with a problem at the outset in a domain totally unfamiliar to students. It appears that in practice there are many instances where this assumption is questionable. There are disciplines and subjects where foundation knowledge is best disseminated first. Effective PBL entails the activation of prior knowledge. Examples of such prior knowledge would be basic principles of physics and mathematical tools. The axioms, language and tools of certain domains are examples of essential prior knowledge. Apart from foundation knowledge, it is important to determine the extent to which problem scenarios should build on and activate prior

> Students' experiences point to the need to prepare learners' mindsets and to ensure good design of problems and of the PBL curriculum. The right level of PBL challenge is important. PBL is successful when we develop students' confidence in independent learning and bring students' learning closer to the real world.

knowledge (Woods, 2000). There is no contradiction in teaching these things first – PBL is not an all-encompassing approach to learning. Hence, PBL problem design must address these two questions: (1) Are there sufficient prior knowl-edge and experience for PBL development to occur? (2) Do the learners have the minimum foundation knowledge, basic tools and language skills as baselines for PBL to have the best leverage?

10

IMPLEMENTATION OF PROBLEM-BASED LEARNING: ADMINISTRATIVE ISSUES

Educational Development with PBL

I was heavily involved in educational and staff development in the last decade as staff developer, manager and director at a higher education institution in Singapore. How effective are educational projects and initiatives? I remember talking to a Harvard-trained and highly experienced World Bank consultant, Dr Chai Hon Chan. He told me that in his more than 20 years of experience and observation of many large-scale educational development projects, funding and resources were not the primary problems. The greatest problem was the lack of project management skills, resulting in the failure to implement good ideas. The management of educational development projects is often taken for granted. Even sadder is the fact that people do not learn from the successes and failures of implementation.

At the International Conference on Problem-based Learning in Higher Education (PBL 2002: A Pathway to Better Learning) hosted by the University of Delaware, the importance of management issues in PBL implementation was given due recognition. John Cavanaugh of the University of North Carolina at Wilmington, John Harris of Samford University, Ann Ferren of Radford University, Mark Huddleston of the University of Delaware and I were asked to discuss issues and strategies for sustaining PBL reforms. Such deliberations are indeed important considering that there are numerous funded PBL projects in many universities worldwide and that many institutions and programmes are keen to adopt PBL approaches. In this final chapter, I shall discuss some of the management issues that PBL champions should note in the course of introducing and implementing PBL educational development projects.

By project we usually mean work that has a beginning and an end rather than processes or routine work that is ongoing. A PBL educational development project entails work that aims to create change in specific aspects of the curriculum and of teaching, learning and assessment. Planning an educational development project begins with the articulation of the objective and the educational benefits that we hope to bring. Also to be elaborated are the rationale, scope, resources and time frame, together with how it will be accomplished, its development monitored and achievement evaluated. Educational development projects involve several phases:

- Preplanning, positioning and definition
- Organization and planning
- Implementation, tracking and monitoring
- Completion and review

These are probably stereotypical stages of most projects. Sometimes it is difficult to define the "completion" stage as such projects are aimed at spearheading a change process that is meant to be ongoing. Nevertheless, completion can be delimited in terms of (1) the time frame for measuring desired outcomes or (2) the duration of funding. What is most important, however, is probably understanding the critical factors that ensure success in each of these stages in bringing about effective change.

Educational innovation has never been easy, whether it is incremental changes in curricula or implementation of alternatives to existing practices (Ford, 1987; Peterson et al., 1997). Pockets of innovations initiated from the ground may not last very long. Projects often have to be top-down as resources tend to be given for rather global and clearly structured projects. It is a sad fact that projects do not always end on a positive note. Speaking of educational reform, Huberman (1989) and Little (1996) observed that more often than not staff involved in institution-wide innovation are disenchanted at the end of such projects. Furthermore, whilst there is sufficient rationale for change, Swann and Pratt (1999) noted that the research conducted to inform change appeared to be less than satisfactory. They observed that, whether in Britain, Australia or the United States, there was a parallel concern that "policy makers do not make good use of research generated by the academic community and others" (p. 3). Morrison (1998) noted that "whilst one can plan for change in a careful way, in practice the plan seldom unfolds in the ways anticipated" (p. 15). He observed that "evolutionary planning" works better than "linear planning".

Case Study of PBL Implementation

The idea of curriculum innovation at the polytechnic where I worked did not happen overnight. As a staff developer, I saw a need for curriculum innovation in terms of moving away from the traditional lecture–tutorial approach to a more learner-centred and active learning approach. Concomitant with the search for more active learning methodology was an increased awareness of the need for change. The viability of a traditional lecture–tutorial system with heavy emphasis on content knowledge had been seriously questioned, but pockets of interactive learning did not seem to satisfy staff nor students. Active learning was emphasized with a view to enhancing thinking and infusing higher-order thinking skills and creativity.

One initiative that caught the attention of management and staff developers at the polytechnic was a pilot programme by a team of computer engineering staff. They came across the concept of PBL and picked up further expertise through study trips and training at the University of Southern Illinois. They adapted the PBL approach in medicine and applied it with enthusiasm to their computer engineering programme. The project caught the attention of management, who immediately saw the potential of using PBL in more polytechnic courses. As I was heading the Thinking Initiative Programme, I saw that PBL philosophy and pedagogy would be useful for anchoring curriculum innovation. The challenge then was taking the idea and growing it into a major project. We seriously needed a project to facilitate further developments, fan into flame the sparks of action, spread the fire and help staff challenge the status quo and promote a shift in the way they looked at teaching and learning. The presence of like-minded PBL champions with the passion and commitment to practise the innovation needed to be supported and recognized.

It was probably on the basis of these macro developments, the initiatives of my colleagues and management support that a PBL approach to polytechnic education was conceived, which eventually led to institution-wide implementation and the establishment of a centre for PBL. The centre was set up "to meet the challenges of preparing students for the world of dynamic change" by adopting "a new academic architecture" that featured PBL (Tan, 2000c). The philosophy of the centre was "to establish a culture of inquiry, enterprise and meaningful student learning" through the use of PBL (Temasek Centre for Problem-based Learning, 2000). It was envisaged that PBL would benefit students in terms of developing problem-solving acumen, multidisciplinary learning and lifelong learning.

Through PBL, students were expected to attain greater self-motivation, develop higher-order thinking skills, teamwork and communication skills (Tan et al., 2000).

The centre provided opportunities for staff from the polytechnic to be trained in PBL through workshops, forums, open lectures and exchanges with PBL experts. The workshops included an introduction to PBL, design of PBL problems, facilitation in PBL, curriculum development in PBL and assessment in PBL. Selected staff were sent to various international PBL centres, such as those at the University of Southern Illinois, University of Maastricht, University of Newcastle, University of Samford, and the Illinois Mathematics and Science Academy. The centre also provided consultation to the various schools of the polytechnic (which then included Design, Business, Engineering, Information Technology, and Applied Science) in curriculum development as well as research and development in PBL. It also collaborated with local and international centres to exchange and advance the practice of PBL. One of its accomplishments was hosting the Second Asia-Pacific Conference on Problem-based Learning, which saw over 140 presentations and some 500 local and overseas delegates.

I was privileged to see the implementation of PBL in a context where the administration and management gave full support and advocated the use of PBL as the anchoring philosophy for professional training and education. The piloting and implementation also won national recognition when a number of colleagues and I won an Innovator Award for co-pioneering PBL as an innovation in education. What was triumphant about the award was not so much our initiatives as educators but the fact that the Enterprise Challenge Unit from the Prime Minister's Office recognized an educational innovation – problem-based learning.

As director of the institution's PBL centre then, I had the opportunity to work with course teams, undertake staff development work and monitor student feedback in PBL initiatives across various disciplines and levels. On reflection, I note two major milestones that epitomize the importance of looking out for and seizing opportunities so that a project can be strategically positioned and be implemented. The first involved an organizational-level strategic planning session where a management retreat was held to "reinvent" polytechnic education. This led to a search for a new academic architecture. The second was the cognizance of the national initiative The Enterprise Challenge (TEC). An educational project did not initially appear to fit the bill as TEC was an "initiative to bring out the Silicon Valley spirit inside the Public Service" and deliverables had to be measurable in terms of cost saving and enterprise of a more inventive nature. In fact, of the seven projects that obtained funding in 2000, six were technology related. One was a biotechnology project that had a direct impact on environment enhancement, two were in information technology and three were in high-technology system design and development. The assessment criteria for TEC award are among the most rigorous of award criteria as it is not only a matter of funding but also the highest recognition of innovation. To present our case for the award, a colleague and I had to appear before a final panel that comprised the Permanent Secretary of the Ministry of Manpower, chief executives from the public and private sectors and senior staff from the Office of the Prime Minister. I had to focus on three things: originality, feasibility and benefits. I was selling a new educational paradigm. I remember being asked what was so original about the idea of PBL. My argument was that it is a revolutionary rather than an evolutionary approach to professional education. It was novel because we intended to have an entire curriculum revamp, changing the way we dealt with content, the mode of delivery, the role of the teacher, the activities of students and the mode of assessment. I made sure I also delimited the project to an area where feasibility and benefits were more realizable.

Positioning, Organization and Planning

PBL educational development projects are aimed at bringing about change and meeting needs. Positioning is an important aspect of such projects, and for a project to be effective it is essential to take note of the following factors:

- *Global trends.* Keep track of global and regional trends that may be related to what you want to implement. They will help you rationalize and define your PBL project.
- *National agenda.* Be aware of national agendas and priorities not only to be politically correct but, more importantly, because a project at the micro level or a small project that fulfils a particular national priority can actually take off much faster than top-down initiatives.
- *Know the state of the art.* Projects should advance the frontiers of knowledge or improve the current state of practice. To bring about such developments, it is important to keep track of the

current status in your field of work and be cognizant of opportunities for innovation.

- *Commitment to change.* Commit to a project for the purpose of advancing good practices or a field of knowledge and take a stand that, whatever changes in policies that may happen, we intend to stick to our commitment. An educational development project, in particular, requires a commitment to change underpinned by sound educational beliefs or philosophy.
- *Beyond educational justification.* Look for more than educational justification because it alone may not convince people. Multi-pronged justifications, such as those with economic or social impact, help.
- *Action research.* Do your own action research (e.g. small-scale collaborative inquiry and improvement studies) and preliminary surveys to support what you plan to do.
- *Consistent championship.* Consistently champion and advance a good idea. PBL projects do not just happen with a one-off idea.
- *Build a team of people.* Project teams can be formed by assignment, but informal collaboration among a group of like-minded people will facilitate the development of the project.
- *Collaborative international network.* Having a network of people locally and internationally who share the same interests can be very helpful, even though they may not be part of the project team.

In addition to these factors, the organization and planning of educational development projects must be based on:

- *Conviction and clarity of purpose.* A strong conviction and a clear idea of PBL and what you want to change help provide the meaning and motivation, without which there would be little momentum for organization and planning.
- *Well-developed ideas and mental models.* It is important to develop a clear idea of the PBL curricula and to formulate mental models for communication.
- *Visualization of the feasibility and benefits.* It helps in project planning to have the end in mind and to visualize the outcomes and benefits.
- *Systems thinking and systematic thinking.* Planning and organization involves constant awareness of the holistic aspect of the project as well as detailed planning.

To implement a major PBL development project, we need high commitment, the right people, focus groups, quality check points and review of progress. The project teams need to be clearly organized with roles and responsibilities defined. Major milestones have to be established with clear time lines and control and monitoring mechanisms.

Paradigm, Process, People and Problems

Whilst planning, systems thinking and systematic thinking help provide the foundation for projects to be effectively started, implementation and sustaining momentum are never easy.

What are the major obstacles? The first pertains to paradigms and mindsets. PBL involves a rather radical change and, whilst its philosophy and rationale seem convincing, people are highly sceptical as they do not know how it will work. I mentioned earlier that the PBL centre at the polytechnic provided staff development in the areas of PBL design, facilitation, curriculum development and assessment. In addition, course teams embarking on PBL worked with PBL staff to develop their curricula. It should be noted, however, that PBL was new to both staff developers and teaching staff. Major gaps in skills were experienced in curriculum design, facilitation and assessment.

The other obstacles are the existing systems and processes. Whilst top-management support may be given, there are often bulky systems already in place that need to be changed. PBL innovation also requires breaking impasse and barriers in many academic policies and systems. For example, the Programme Validation Committee and the Senate have to be consulted when major changes in curriculum or in modes of assessment are involved. Going through these major committees means that things would be slowed down tremendously. There are also the educational quality assurance systems and standard student feedback forms designed to assess the effectiveness of lectures and tutorials. The lecturer's roles in PBL are very different. The standard student feedback form includes items like "clarity of explanation", but PBL entails getting students to seek and obtain their own solutions and explanations. The approach we adopted was educating and helping peers become informed.

All projects aim to achieve the objectives and benefits within budget, on schedule and with the desired quality through effective definition, organization and planning, execution, tracking, managing of problems, and completion. The completion of a PBL project may be defined in terms of a full cycle of PBL implementation for a particular academic year. The polytechnic in question incidentally also employs total quality management. Because PBL was prescribed as a useful alternative, surveys of lecturers' perceptions generally showed a positive response. However, surveys and monitoring of student feedback produced mixed results. Whilst quantitative data were helpful for a broad picture, the most valuable sources of insights were qualitative. I have given some case vignettes of students in the previous chapter (see also Tan, 2001). From the perspective of educational development project management, what insights and lessons can we draw from a review of the processes, interactions and outcomes?

The Uncertainty Principle

In a culture where planning and systematic thinking prevail, the very strength of project planning becomes a major weakness. I learnt the hard way about what we may call the uncertainty principle of PBL project management. When we try to locate where we are on the time line of project completion, often we are unsure of the momentum, namely, how and where it is heading and with what intensity! Thus, in PBL all we know is that we are practising things characteristic of PBL, but we are really not very sure if we are achieving the intended outcomes. As noted earlier, even assessment systems have to be changed because we are not measuring the same things as before. The presence of such uncertainties, however, does not necessarily depreciate the value of the project. Accepting the uncertainty principle is a necessary part of educational project management, in particular PBL projects.

Practical and Systems Barriers

The experiences with PBL point to the fact that de-skilling and re-skilling are essential to PBL innovations. The lack of PBL skills (e.g. problem design, coaching, curriculum development) was one factor responsible for many implementation problems. Apart from skills, related problems are often the lack of resources such as time, administrative support, space and materials. Besides all the planning, PBL resources for students, the design of problems, availability of rooms for PBL-type discussions, and support staff are important concerns. Sometimes staff can be caught in a vicious cycle where the lack of time, support and resources leads to poor quality from stage to stage. Sometimes the systems in place do not support change. In fact, the more efficient the current system, the greater it is a barrier to change. Thus, if the educational quality assurance system has been developed and fine-tuned over a period of time for a lecture–tutorial system, it is never easy to dismantle the system quickly to cater to the PBL approach. Yet, the quality system will inevitably be tied to staff appraisal systems and course evaluation systems. Clearly, a single project of educational change is not normally conceived with immediate consideration of existing systems. The only solution is flexibility on the part of the custodians of these systems, and it is here that project leaders have to win collaboration and promote ownership of new ideas through strategic communication.

Mindset and Value Barriers

PBL implementation involves mindset change in academic staff and students as well as administration. People naturally feel more secure, comfortable and confident with familiar ways of teaching and learning, and changes are bound to be initially resisted. As mentioned earlier, staff training and plenty of preparation are needed to overcome psychological barriers. There are, however, deeper barriers that are sometimes difficult to penetrate. On issues of teaching and learning, one will find that the barriers pertaining to value and belief systems go deeper than psychological barriers. Resistance sometimes results in paying lip service or "conspiracy of the least", namely, doing just enough to get by. There are no easy solutions to such resistance; the positive approach is to establish success cases to convince people of the true value and benefit of the project. This is why recruiting champions for a project is important for it to take off.

The Whole is More than the Sum of Its Parts

PBL projects tend to experience student resistance in the initial stages of implementation. If we rely on initial responses alone to decide whether to proceed with PBL, it would never take off. Similarly, many parts of a system may not be optimized when change is happening. A holistic approach and a systems perspective are more helpful in addressing the diverse barriers and the problems that crop up.

Whilst the technicalities of planning, scheduling, resource allocation, prioritizing and so on are important, the factors that make a project work are people collaboration and ownership. The same approach that we use to facilitate PBL lessons should be practised in PBL implementation.

PBL implementation involves change initiatives, which are iterative in nature and spiral in development. The same processes often have to be revisited and the outcomes are but the beginning of another iterative process. Good management of PBL educational development projects is about championing a desired change that is rooted in much informed deliberation and planning. It is about challenging the status quo and taking risks while being aware of both global developments and the localized contexts.

EPILOGUE

More than two millennia ago, the Greek thinker Aristotle believed that knowledge begins with experience. The mind, according to Aristotle, is what gives the "intuitive leap" from uncertainty to knowledge. The word *knowledge*, which is *epistemê* in Greek, is translated as *scientia* in Latin. The 21st century is often described as the knowledge-based era. Knowledge is growing at an ever-increasing speed. However, it is fragmenting just as fast and will continue to do so if we do not know how to integrate learning from different disciplines and develop strategies for deep learning of things new and important to us. Knowledge takes on a new dimension today. We need a new science of looking at knowledge and information; we also need a new art of learning.

Problem-based approaches are about learning to confront an ill-structured situation – a situation where we are uncertain about data, information and solution – and mastering the art of intuitive leap. That is why in PBL processes the mind of the learner is the focus of the tutor. We make our thinking and mind visible through dialogue. The Greek word for dialogue is *dia-logos*. *Logos* refers to the making of meaning. PBL is about creating meaningful learning through inquiry and through a rich variety and channels of dialogue. Through collegial critique, self-evaluation and reflection, we sharpen our mental tools in problem solving. We repeatedly talk about PBL cycles and stages, such as the identification of problems and the analysis and hypothesis stages. In the real world today, many poor decisions and undesirable consequences are a result of the failure to collect and establish facts. We emphasize systematic thinking and logical thinking. In the analysis and hypothesis stages, PBL students learn through a process of conjectures and refutations. Unlike traditional problem solving, where students tend to work towards the verification of a standard solution, PBL takes a more open approach. Sometimes justification is also done through what Karl Popper (1972), the well-known philosopher of science, called a "falsification" process – dealing with what is not and arriving at a cluster of possible alternatives. This calls for not only analytical thinking but also analogy and imagination in presenting possible solutions in a variety of "what if" contexts. In *The Logic of Scientific Discovery*, Popper argued that it is imagination and creativity, not induction, that generate real scientific theories. My own research in cognition, built on the works of Robert Sternberg and Reuven Feuerstein, has convinced me that good problem solvers employ a wide range of cognitive functions and use multiple thinking tools and processes. Robert and Michele Root-Bernstein (1999) rightly observed in *Sparks of Genius* that:

> *we feel what we know and know what we feel. This kind of understanding depends upon an integrated use of thinking tools such that, first, we synthesize sensory impressions and feelings and, second, we fuse our sensory synthesis with the abstract knowledge that exists in our memories as patterns, models, analogies, and other higher-order mental constructs. Many gifted individuals thus work toward synthetic understanding by purposely cultivating a multiple-sensing of the world (pp. 297–8).*

I hope that through the ideas, suggestions and approaches put forward in this book you will attempt to use problems and PBL processes to encourage cross-disciplinary learning as well as multiple ways of learning and thinking.

Just as Milo learnt in *The Phantom Tollbooth* that *the only failure is not to try*, we should be adventurous in our use of problems to power learning in the 21st century.

USEFUL WEB SITES ON PROBLEM-BASED LEARNING

This appendix lists some of the most useful Internet resources on PBL. The list is by no means exhaustive, but these are the sites of institutions where major PBL initiatives and projects have taken place and are ongoing. The purpose of this selection is to give the reader an idea of how PBL has been used at different levels worldwide. These sites also provide examples of how PBL is used in different disciplines and levels of education.

www.udel.edu/pbl

This Web site of the University of Delaware is particularly useful for PBL in higher education. It features a PBL Clearinghouse that offers access to a range of PBL problems in various disciplines. The site provides many useful articles for new PBL practitioners as well as PBL researchers, together with useful links to other major PBL Web sites. It also offers ideas for problems in the sciences, humanities and cross-disciplinary learning at advanced and higher education levels.

www.samford.edu/pbl/pbl_main.html

This Web site of the University of Samford provides a glossary of information about PBL. It has an excellent PBL Peer Review Online portfolio, which features PBL practitioners' reflections pertaining to the design of PBL courses, student learning and overall evaluation.

www.imsa.edu/team/cpbl/cpbl.html

This Web site of the Center for Problem-based Learning of the Illinois Mathematics and Science Academy provides a good introduction to PBL. It also has good examples of problems for K–12 curriculum levels. It is particularly relevant for secondary school teachers interested in using science-related issues for their PBL curricula.

http://pbli.org

This is the Web site of the Problem-based Learning Initiative group of teachers and researchers engaged in PBL and staff development. Hosted by the Department of Medical Education of the Southern Illinois University School of Medicine, it provides an introduction to using PBL across various disciplines and educational levels.

www.d261.k12.id.us/Technology/Goals%202000/PBL/problem_based_learning.htm

This Web site of the Jerome School District in Idaho provides many examples of PBL projects in elementary, junior high and high schools. Each project comprises directions for teachers and students together with clear examples of guides and templates for problem statements, lists of problems, identification of resources, management process and assessment rubrics. Primary and secondary school teachers will find this site helpful for getting ideas on infusing PBL in science and social science subjects.

www.mcli.dist.maricopa.edu/pbl/info.html

The PBL material developed by the Maricopa Community Colleges offers useful examples of using PBL to develop problem-solving skills in many day-to-day challenges and decision making. There is a good project on PBL in mathematics (e.g. a problem on buying a car). The PBL manuals provide teachers with useful tips on how to organize and start PBL curricula.

http://meds-ss10.meds.queensu.ca/medicine/pbl/pblhome.htm

This PBL homepage of the School of Medicine of Queen's University in Ontario, Canada, provides a good example of how PBL is used in health sciences and how one can set up PBL support, student's guides, tutor's guides, PBL links and resources.

www.tp.edu.sg/pblconference/advcomm.html

This is the homepage of the Second Asia-Pacific Conference on Problem-based Learning. The 2000 conference theme was PBL: Education Innovation across Disciplines. The post-conference proceedings are posted here and comprise a range of papers on PBL in disciplines such as medicine, health sciences, nursing, engineering, law, business, literature and education.

BIBLIOGRAPHY

Achilles, C.M., & Hoover, S.P. (1996). *Problem-based learning (PBL) as a school-improvement vehicle*. ERIC Document Reproduction Service No. ED 401 631.

Albanese, M., & Mitchell, S. (1993). PBL: A review of the literature on its outcomes and implementation issues. *Academic Medicine, 68,* 52–81.

Armstrong, E.G. (1991). A hybrid model of PBL. In D. Boud & G. Feletti (Eds), *The challenge of problem-based learning*. London: Kogan Page.

Arons, A.B. (1978). Teaching science. In S.M. Cahn (Ed.), *Scholars who teach: The art of college teaching* (pp. 101–30). Chicago: Nelson-Hall.

Balla, J.I. (1990a). Insights into some aspects of clinical education, I: Clinical practice. *Postgraduate Medical Journal, 66,* 212–17.

Balla, J.I. (1990b). Insights into some aspects of clinical education, II: A theory for clinical education. *Postgraduate Medical Journal, 66,* 297–301.

Barrows, H. (1986). A taxonomy of PBL methods. *Medical Education, 20,* 481–6.

Barrows, H.S., & Tamblyn, R.M. (1980). *Problem-based learning: An approach to medical education*. New York: Springer.

Berkson, L. (1993). PBL: Have the expectations been met? *Academic Medicine, 68,* 79–88.

Biggs, J. (1996). Enhancing teaching through constructive alignment. *Higher Education, 32,* 1–18.

Bok, D. (1993). *The cost of talent: How executives and professionals are paid and how it affects America.* New York: Free Press.

Boud, D., & Feletti, G.I. (Eds) (1997). *The challenge of problem-based learning,* 2nd ed. London: Kogan Page.

Bourne, L.E. Jr, Dominowski, R.L., & Loftus, E.F. (1979). *Cognitive processes.* Englewood Cliffs, NJ: Prentice Hall.

Bray, J., Lee, J., Smith, L., & Yorks, L. (2000). *Collaborative inquiry in practice. Action, reflection, and making meaning.* London: Sage.

Brennan, J., Fedrowitz, J., Huber, M., & Shah, T. (1999). *What kind of university? International perspectives on knowledge, participation and governance.* Buckingham; Philadelphia, PA: Society for Research into Higher Education and Open University Press.

Bridges, E.M., & Hallinger, P. (1995). *Implementing problem based learning in leadership development.* Eugene, OR: ERIC Clearinghouse on Educational Management, University of Oregon.

Bruner, J. (1960). *The process of education.* Cambridge, MA: Harvard University Press.

Carlson, H. (1999). From practice to theory: A social constructivist approach to teacher education. *Teachers and Teaching: Theory and Practice, 5,* 203–18.

Chen, A.Y., & Tan, O.S. (2002). Towards a blended design for e-learning. *Centre for Development of Teaching and Learning Brief, 5,* 6–8.

Chi, M.T.H., & Glaser, R. (1985). Problem solving ability. In R.J. Sternberg (Ed.), *Human abilities: An information processing approach* (pp. 227–50). New York: Freeman.

Chi, M.T.H., Siler, S.A., Jeong, H., Yamauchi, T., & Hausmann, R. (2001). Learning from human tutoring. *Cognitive Science, 25,* 471–533.

Chin, C.A., & Brewer, W.F. (2001). Models of data: A theory of how people evaluate data. *Cognition and Instruction, 19,* 323–51.

Cuban, L. (1999). *How scholars trumped teachers: Change without reform in university curriculum, teaching, and research, 1890–1990.* New York: Teachers College Press.

Delisle, R. (1997). *How to use problem-based learning in the classroom.* Alexandria, VA: Association for Supervision and Curriculum Development.

Dewey, J. (1963). *Experience and education.* New York: Simon & Schuster.

Diamond, R.M. (1989). *Designing and improving courses and curricula in higher education: A systematic approach.* San Francisco: Jossey-Bass.

Economic Development Board (1999). *A knowledge-based economy.* Singapore.

Eraut, M. (1994). *Developing professional knowledge and competence.* London: Falmer Press.

Evans, J.B.T., Venn, S., & Feeney, A. (2002). Implicit and explicit processes in a hypothesis testing task. *British Journal of Psychology, 93,* 31–46.

Feuerstein, R. (1990). The theory of structural modifiability. In B. Presseisen (Ed.), *Learning and thinking styles: Classroom interaction.* Washington, DC: National Education Association.

Feuerstein, R., & Feuerstein, S. (1991). Mediated learning experience: A theoretical review. In R. Feuerstein, P.S. Klein & A.J. Tannenbaum (Eds), *Mediated learning experience (MLE): Theoretical, psychosocial and learning implications* (pp. 3–51). London: Freund.

Ford, S. (1987). *Evaluating educational innovation.* New York: Croom Helm.

Gallagher, S.A., Stepien, W.J., & Rosenthal, H. (1992). The effects of PBL on problem solving. *Gifted Child Quarterly, 36,* 195–200.

Gardner, H. (1983). *Frames of mind: The theory of multiple intelligences.* New York: Basic Books.

Gijselaers, W.H. (1996). Connecting problem-based practices with educational theory. In L.A. Wilkerson & W.H. Gijselaers (Eds), *Bringing problem-based learning to higher education: Theory and practice* (pp. 13–21). San Francisco: Jossey-Bass.

Glasgow, N.A. (1997). *New curriculum for new times: A guide to student-centered, problem-based learning.* Thousand Oaks, CA: Corwin Press.

Handy, C. (1994). *The empty raincoat: Making sense of the future.* London: Hutchinson.

Hargreaves, A. (1994). *Changing teachers, changing times.* London: Cassell.

Hendry, G.D., & Murphy, L.B. (1995). Constructivism and problem-based learning. In P. Little, M. Ostwald & G. Ryan (Eds), *Research and development in problem-based learning, 3: Assessment and evaluation.* Newcastle: Australian Problem Based Learning Network.

Hicks, M.J. (1991). *Problem solving in business and management: Hard, soft and creative approaches.* London: International Thomson Business Press.

Huberman, M. (1989). The professional life cycle of teachers. *Teachers College Record, 91,* 31–57.

Knapper, C.K., & Cropley, A.J. (Eds) (1991). *Lifelong learning and higher education,* 2nd ed. London: Kogan Page.

Knowles, M.S. (1980). *The modern practice of adult education: From pedagogy to andragogy.* Chicago: Follett.

Kuhn, T.S. (1962). *The structure of scientific revolutions.* Chicago: University of Chicago Press.

Lee, F.J., & Anderson, J.R. (2001). Does learning a complex task have to be complex? A study in learning decomposition. *Cognitive Psychology, 42,* 267–316.

Little, J.W. (1996). The emotional contours and career trajectories of (disappointed) reform enthusiasts. *Cambridge Journal of Education, 26,* 345–59.

Little, P., Tan, O.S., Kandlbinder, P., Williams, A., Cleary, K., & Conway, J. (Eds) (2001). *On problem based learning: Experience, empowerment and evidence.* Proceedings of the 3rd Asia Pacific Conference on Problem Based Learning. Newcastle: Australian Problem Based Learning Network. www.newcastle.edu.au/conferences/PBL2001.

Manktelow, K.I. (1999). *Reasoning and thinking.* Hove, East Sussex: Psychology Press.

Margetson, D. (1994). Current educational reform and the significance of PBL. *Studies in Higher Education, 19,* 5–19.

Marincovich, M. (2000). Problems and promises in problem-based learning. In O.S. Tan, P. Little, S.Y. Hee & J. Conway (Eds), *Problem-based learning: Educational innovation across disciplines* (pp. 3–11). Singapore: Temasek Centre for Problem-based Learning.

Mayer, R.E. (1983). *Thinking, problem solving and cognition.* New York: Freeman.

Ministry of Education (1998). *The desired outcomes of education.* Singapore.

Ministry of Manpower (1999). *Manpower 21: Vision of a talent capital.* Singapore.

Ministry of Trade and Industry (1998). *Committee on Singapore Competitiveness.* Singapore.

Morrison, K. (1998). *Management theories for educational change.* London: Paul Chapman.

National Research Council (1999). *How people learn: Bridging research and practice.* Washington, DC: National Academy Press.

National University of Singapore (2000). Selected results from 2 CDTL surveys. *CDTLink, 4*(2), 12. National University of Singapore Centre for Development of Teaching and Learning.

Norman, G.R., & Schmidt, H.G. (1992). The psychological basis of problem-based learning: A review of the evidence. *Academic Medicine, 67,* 557–65.

Norman, G.R., & Schmidt, H.G. (2000). Effectiveness of problem-based learning curricula. *Medical Education, 34,* 721–8.

Oliva, P.F. (1992). *Developing the curriculum.* New York: HarperCollins.

Parkay, F.W., & Hass, G. (2000). *Curriculum planning: A contemporary approach,* 7th ed. Boston: Allyn & Bacon.

Peterson, M.W., Dill, D.D., Mets, L.A., & associates (1997). *Planning and management for a changing environment: A handbook on redesigning postsecondary institutions.* San Francisco: Jossey-Bass.

Polya, G. (1990). *How to solve it,* 2nd ed. London: Penguin.

Popper, K. (1972). *The logic of scientific discovery.* London: Hutchinson.

Popper, K.R. (1992). *Unended quest.* London: Routledge.

Ramsden, P. (1998). *Learning to lead in higher education.* New York: Routledge.

Robinson, V. (1993). *Problem-based methodology: Research for the improvement of practice.* Oxford: Pergamon Press.

Root-Bernstein, R., & Root-Bernstein, M. (1999). *Sparks of genius: The thirteen thinking tools of the world's most creative people.* Boston, MA: Houghton Mifflin.

Savery, J.R., & Duffy, T.M. (1995). PBL: Instructional model and its constructivist framework. *Educational Technology, 35,* 31–7.

Savin-Baden, M. (2000). *Problem-based learning in higher education: Untold stories.* Buckingham; Philadelphia, PA: Society for Research into Higher Education and Open University Press.

Schlechty, P. (1990). *Schools for the twenty-first century.* San Francisco: Jossey-Bass.

Schmidt, H.G. (1993). Foundations of problem-based learning: Some explanatory notes. *Medical Education, 27,* 422–432.

Schon, D.A. (1983). *The reflective practitioner: How professionals think in action.* New York: Basic Books.

Schwartz, P., Mennin, S., & Webb, G. (2001). *Problem based learning: Case studies, experience and practice.* London: Kogan Page.

Shulman, L.S. (1991). Pedagogical ways of knowing. Keynote address delivered at the International Council on Education for Teaching (ICET) 1990 World Assembly, Singapore. Singapore: Institute of Education.

Stepien, W.J., & Gallagher, S.A. (1993). Problem-based learning: As authentic as it gets. *Educational Leadership, 50,* 25–8.

Sternberg, R.J. (1985). Approaches to intelligence. In S.F. Chipman, J.W. Segal & R. Glaser (Eds), *Thinking and learning skills,* Vol. 2: *Research and open questions.* Hillsdale, NJ: Erlbaum.

Sternberg, R.J. (1986). *Intelligence applied: Understanding and increasing your intellectual skills.* San Diego, CA: Harcourt Brace Jovanovich.

Sternberg, R.J. (1990). *Metaphors of mind: Conceptions of the nature of intelligence.* New York: Cambridge University Press.

Sternberg, R.J., & Davidson, J.E. (Eds) (1995). *The nature of insight.* Cambridge, MA: MIT Press.

Straits Times (1997). R-Adm Teo: Gear up for thinking schools. 31 July, p. 1.

Straits Times (2002). Major overhaul needed, not just small changes. 27 November, p. H2.

Swann, J., & Pratt, J. (Eds) (1999). *Improving education: Realist approach to method and research.* New York: Cassell.

Tan, O.S. (1994). Curriculum development for the 21st century: A model and perspective for course designers. *Temasek Journal,* July, pp. 34–41.

Tan, O.S. (1996). World trends in higher education: The Singapore and Southeast Asian context. Keynote address delivered at the 7th Annual Conference of the International Students Advisers' Network of Australia. Adelaide, December.

Tan, O.S. (1999). Productivity, employability and sustainability: A Singapore perspective. Keynote address delivered at National Careers Agenda: Keys to the Development of a Nation. Brunei, June.

Tan, O.S. (2000a). Effects of a cognitive modifiability intervention on cognitive abilities, attitudes and academic performance of polytechnic students. PhD thesis, National Institute of Education, Nanyang Technological University, Singapore.

Tan, O.S. (2000b). Intelligence enhancement and cognitive coaching in problem-based learning. In C.M. Wang, K.P. Mohanan, D. Pan & Y.S. Chee (Eds), *TLHE Symposium Proceedings*. Singapore: National University of Singapore.

Tan, O.S. (2000c). Reflecting on innovating the academic architecture for the 21st century. *Educational Developments, 1,* 8–11.

Tan, O.S. (2000d). Thinking skills, creativity and problem-based learning. In O.S. Tan, P. Little, S.Y. Hee & J. Conway (Eds), *Problem-based learning: Educational innovation across disciplines* (pp. 47–55). Singapore: Temasek Centre for Problem-based Learning.

Tan, O.S. (2001). PBL innovation: An institution-wide implementation and students' experiences. In P. Little, O.S. Tan, P. Kandlbinder, A. Williams, K. Cleary & J. Conway (Eds), *On problem based learning: Experience, empowerment and evidence.* Proceedings of the 3rd Asia Pacific Conference on Problem Based Learning (pp. 318–33). Newcastle: Australian Problem Based Learning Network.

Tan, O.S. (2002a). Enhancing higher education in the knowledge-based era through problem-based learning approaches. Keynote address delivered at the International Conference on University Learning and Teaching: Issues and Challenges (InCULT2002). Shah Alam, Selangor, Malaysia, October.

Tan, O.S. (2002b). Lifelong learning through a problem-based learning approach. In A.S.C. Chang & C.C.M. Goh (Eds), *Teachers' handbook on teaching generic thinking skills* (pp. 22–36). Singapore: Prentice Hall.

Tan, O.S. (2002c). Problem-based learning: More problems for teacher education. *Review of Educational Research and Advances for Classroom Teachers*, 21, 43–55.

Tan, O.S. (2002d). Project management in educational development: A Singapore experience. In M. Yorke, P. Martin & C. Baume (Eds), *Managing educational development projects: Maximising impact* (pp. 153–70). London: Kogan Page.

Tan, O.S. (2002e). Knowledge and participation reconsidered: Some implications for teaching and learning. *aCEDemia*, 1, 3–4.

Tan, O.S., Little, P., Hee, S.Y., & Conway, J. (Eds) (2000). *Problem-based learning: Educational innovation across disciplines.* Singapore: Temasek Centre for Problem-based Learning.

Tan, O.S., Parsons, R.D., Hinson, S.L., & Sardo-Brown, D. (2003). *Educational psychology: A practitioner–researcher approach (An Asian edition).* Singapore: Thomson Learning.

Tan, O.S., & Yap, Y. (1991–93). *Mathematics: A problem-solving approach*, vols 1–3. Singapore: Federal Publications.

Temasek Centre for Problem-based Learning (2000). *Temasek Centre for Problem-based Learning.* Singapore: Temasek Polytechnic.

Trop, L., & Sage, S. (1998). *Problems as possibilities: Problem-based learning for K–12 education.* Alexandria, VA: Association for Supervision and Curriculum Development.

Vernon, D.T., & Blake, R.L. (1993). Does PBL work? A meta-analysis of evaluative research. *Academic Medicine*, 68, 550–60.

Welber, M. (2002). *Where we've been and where we're going: A look at the future of e-learning.* www.elearningmag.com/elearning/article/articleDetail.jsp?id=6703.

West, S.A. (1992). Problem-based learning: A viable addition for secondary school science. *School Science Review*, 73, 47–55.

West, L.H.T., & Pines, A.L. (Eds) (1985). Cognitive structure and conceptual change. New York: Academic Press.

Woods, D.R. (2000). Helping your students gain the most from PBL. In O.S. Tan, P. Little, S.Y. Hee & J. Conway (Eds), *Problem-based learning: Educational innovation across disciplines.* Singapore: Temasek Centre for Problem-based Learning.